second edition

Principles

of

Singing

A TEXTBOOK
FOR VOICE CLASS OR STUDIO

Kenneth E. Miller

University of Missouri—St. Louis

Prentice Hall

Library of Congress Cataloging-in-Publication Data

Miller, Kenneth E.
    Principles of singing : a text book for voice class or studio
  Kenneth E. Miller. -- 2nd ed.
      p.   cm.
    ISBN 0-13-712712-X
    1. Singing--Instruction and study.   I. Title.
  MT820.M598 1990
  783'.0071--dc20

                                              89-38270
                                                CIP
                                                MN

Editorial/production supervision and
  interior design: Carole R. Crouse
Manufacturing buyer: Raymond Keating/Michael Woerner

Printed in the United States of America

10 9 8 7 6 5 4

ISBN 0-13-712712-X

Prentice-Hall International (UK) Limited, London
Prentice-Hall of Australia Pty. Limited, Sydney
Prentice-Hall Canada Inc., Toronto
Prentice-Hall Hispanoamericana, S.A., Mexico
Prentice-Hall of India Private Limited, New Delhi
Prentice-Hall of Japan, Inc., Tokyo
Pearson Education Asia Pte. Ltd., Singapore
Editoria Prentice-Hall do Brasil, Ltda., Rio De Janeiro

Contents

Contents

Preface

Principles of Singing, organized in a series of eighteen units, is written for use in the initial stage of your voice study. This volume contains the most needed principles, exercises, and vocalises plus valuable and interesting songs. Whether you are singing in studio, class, or chorus, you'll find here the tools you need. You can profit by studying each unit, by practicing the exercises and vocalises, and, later, by singing those songs appropriate to your particular voice.

The development of your full potential for singing is a process that may take many years, and you may go through several stages of development. But the first months of study are of particular importance; it is then that you will begin to master those fundamental principles and techniques that will serve you during your entire career.

Written explanations, exercises, vocalises, and song repertoire are pointed out specifically to those of you who have already had some experience with music notation but who now wish to develop your vocal capability. That ability may lead you ultimately to perform professionally, as a solo singer in your own community, or as a more experienced choral musician. Whatever your goal, the information contained here will give you the tools necessary for its realization. The first steps toward improved vocal habits are the same for all adult singers.

If you are to achieve your goal, you should have a clear idea of your vocal art. It must be understood that singing involves both music and text. If any singer does not work to develop either of these two areas fully, the total performance will suffer. This point may appear to be obvious, but the fact is that singers generally work to improve their vocal tones more than their performance of the text. Your own goal should be to give equal importance to the text.

As a student, you should be aware that some aspects of singing rely on mental preparation, while others require physical preparation. For example, it is of primary importance for you both to maintain good physical posture at all times and to prepare mentally before singing.

Each topic covered in this text includes a comprehensive discussion of pertinent information, but the specific points are discussed as briefly and as clearly as possible. All significant previous publications in the field have been reviewed as a part of this research, and there are numerous references to the ideas of other singers, teachers, and writers. The information presented has been used successfully by many leading teachers of singing and by choral conductors.

Practical information is included on such topics as the development of a singer, starting and stopping the tone, the importance of a free tone, legato and sustained tones, vowels, consonants, and studio and public appearances. Each topic includes definite points that will be applicable to the development of any singer.

Although it is important to include exercises and vocalises in the practice period, you should keep in mind that your ultimate goal is to sing songs. The repertoire included in this book has been selected for use by the young singer. Because it is assumed that any basic problems in musicianship will have been corrected by a teacher, that topic will not be addressed here. But it is appropriate to include some brief information about the need for a good musical ear.

The mature singer develops an ability to "feel" a free and natural tone, but the beginner must rely largely on a teacher for such discrimination. It may take several weeks or months for you to be able to judge your own "good" and "bad" tones consistently. A good musical ear and a clear mental image of the sound desired will be quite helpful. When you can begin to know the difference between your "good" and "bad" tones, you can begin to sing with consistency, and you will progress more rapidly.

It is important that you have a genuine interest in improving your singing. Without your own full participation, your progress will be less rapid. Progress toward perfecting your singing does not depend entirely on an intellectual understanding of the principles involved. Such an understanding is important, but it is also necessary for you to apply consistently the knowledge acquired. Neither is it enough for you to have a simple desire to sing; such a desire is important, but it must be backed by adequate information and practice. Your improvement as a singer will be most rapid and solid when you combine a desire to sing with a consistent application of the principles involved. The objectives of this book are to give you the information you need, first, to understand how to progress, and second, to be able to use the exercises, vocalises, and songs to improve your singing. It will be most helpful for you to study with a teacher, but many principles can be applied with little supervision.

You should begin by singing the vocal exercises included at the close of each unit. Even if you have already had considerable singing experience, you should give yourself time to increase your understanding of the singing process by repeating those exercises regularly. If you are to improve as you should, it will be necessary for you to refine your vocal habits, and that refinement can take place more quickly if you do not try to sing too much repertoire too soon. After you begin to develop a feeling for your better vocal tones, you should expand your singing to include the repertoire chosen for your use.

You need to use your voice without forcing if you are to produce increasingly refined vocal tones, and the use of a mirror can help you detect any unusual physical mannerisms or bad habits. For example, if your facial muscles are tense, your vocal tones may have a tendency to be constricted. You should try to avoid any body tension of this kind. Much time can be saved if such problems are detected early.

You will be well advised not to sing when you have a sore throat, but you can use your practice time quite profitably by studying the music silently. In so doing, your emphasis should be on studying the music; silently mouthing the words is not recommended. This kind of practice places your entire attention on the music and results in increased musical understanding. Also, you should practice the exercises and songs often enough to commit them to memory. Having memorized the music, you will be free to focus your attention on your singing. Many singers find that it takes them longer to memorize the text than the music; if that is true for you, it may be helpful for you to begin early to study the text alone.

TO THE TEACHER

You may teach students in a studio, in a voice class, or in a chorus; this text will be useful in any of those situations. Of course, the way you approach a class will be different from the way you approach an individual student. For example, students in a class can work together to their mutual advantage; they can learn from one another. However, there should always be time allotted for singing individually.

Many teachers consider some combination of individual and group instruction to be best.

Both the student and the teacher must realize that the first step toward becoming a mature singer is for the student to understand and use correct vocal habits. It is sometimes necessary for a beginning student to unlearn faulty concepts before real progress can be made, and the information presented here covers major problems often encountered when working with the singer.

The repertoire included has been chosen with the help of other voice teachers and musicians who work with students. There is repertoire suitable for each voice classification, and the music has been chosen especially for its variety and suitability for the beginning singer. This singer may be in a high school, college, university, conservatory, or private studio. The information presented may be consumed by an adult singer within a relatively short time, but you may expect a beginning student to profit from a year or more of study.

Students often want to know their voice classifications as soon as possible, and you can sometimes give a general assessment of their capabilities quite soon. However, you are encouraged not to give firm answers until the student has worked long enough for you to be certain the mature voice has emerged. Any hard information you give about the student's voice classification before you are quite certain you have heard the real voice may have to be changed later.

Beginning students will profit from supervision. The exercises they sing should be simple, clear, and easily committed to memory. When the student begins to sing art songs, the exercises should be related to the repertoire being sung. Beginning students should be assigned a variety of activities in their lessons, and the order of the lesson should be changed often. This will help to keep the lesson interesting and the student always alert. Variety, stimulation, and the ability of the teacher to adapt to individual differences among the students will help to make voice lessons more interesting and beneficial.

Considerable progress has been made in scientific investigation of the vocal mechanism. Carefully documented findings in the studies of anatomy, physiology, and acoustics are presented here. Of equal importance is the practical experience of teachers in the field, of students, of professional musicians. The ideas presented in *Principles of Singing* are derived from all of those sources, along with my own experience.

Many significant changes are included in the second edition: There are new songs, and most songs are for high and low voice ranges; several new vocal exercises have been included; the written information has been revised; and Dr. Bastian has written very informative new material concerning the care of the voice. The result has been to make this second edition much more useful to singers in a voice class, studio, or chorus.

Kenneth E. Miller

1 *The Development of a Singer*

Most experienced singers say they never stop learning, and beginning students are just beginning their development. One basic assumption of almost any kind of education is that inexperienced students can receive valuable guidance from more experienced teachers. In singing, such guidance is especially helpful. A singer who has already progressed beyond the first stages of singing can be expected to give young students the benefit of that first-hand experience.

It should be understood that there is no single set of qualifications necessary to become a fine singer. But there are basic qualifications without which it will be more difficult to become an experienced, artistic performer. Those desirable qualifications form the basis of the discussion in this unit.

MUSICIANSHIP

Any student must be able to read simple music notation before starting to study singing. Otherwise, a teacher of singing will have to devote too much time to the teaching of general musicianship. It is recommended that every student take time to secure that information, which can be acquired in any of the following ways: through classes in musicianship, by studying piano or another instrument, by participation in a choral or an instrumental performing ensemble, or by independent study of music notation.

It is no longer possible for you to excel in the art of singing just because you possess an unusually fine natural vocal instrument; such a singer could possibly have been successful in a career some years ago, but musical training and well-developed musical instincts now are also necessary for any solo or choral singer to be really successful.

It is also important for you to develop a keen musical ear in your first year of study. Although it may not be possible for every student to have had formal classes in ear training before starting the study of singing, it is important for every singer to possess an ability to discriminate between "good" and "bad" musical sounds. Your own progress depends as much on this ability as on any other aspect of your training.

It will be helpful for you to possess a particular kind of musical ear. The singer needs "to imagine accurately (that is, to hear mentally) pitches or musical sounds and to reproduce the imagined pitches by . . . humming or singing."[1] It is not enough for you to be able to imagine pitches accurately; although that is an important step, little will have been gained if you cannot also sing those sounds accurately with your own voice.

[1]Sergius Kagen, *On Studying Singing* (New York: Dover, 1950), p. 8.

1

Of course, every performing musician needs to have a clear sense of musical rhythm. A metronome can be helpful in some situations, but it is best for your rhythmic sense to come from within you. Such an inner rhythmic sense will serve as a permanent musical resource on which you can call, and it will give you a greater sense of musical security.

The importance of rhythm in music has often been discussed, and it cannot be emphasized too much. Students who have fine voice potential but little or no sense of musical rhythm will be unable to sing musically. However, students who have an ability to read music notation, a keen musical ear, and an inner sense of musical rhythm will have a solid sense of musicianship to complement whatever vocal capability they may possess.

PHYSICAL DEVELOPMENT

Knowing the age and the physical development of a singer can be important in trying to predict future success, for "it is difficult to predict the future of a student, especially if he is young."[2]

An adolescent should not be expected to sing with the same fully developed tone that may be expected of a singer who is a few years older. It is possible to begin the study of singing at such an early age that the time may be better spent in the study of piano or another instrument, for the study of a musical instrument can be an important aid in building basic musicianship. But age is only one of several points to consider when making a prediction about a singer's future success.

Every experienced teacher has heard voices of young people who sound as if they could be several years older. These are unusual, naturally well developed young voices, and it is generally such talents that have a chance at a future professional singing career. But the large majority of singing students do not possess such special ability. Most singers in their early adolescent years will not sing with as fully developed sound as they will be able to use when they are several years older. It is simply a matter of physical maturity, and the degree of maturity needs to be taken into account when a teacher gives advice to a young singer about possible future aspirations. It is important not to take advantage of talented young singers by pressing them into advanced singing too soon. A wise and experienced teacher can be invaluable in knowing what to do (and what not to do) in such a situation.

Physical stature can be important to the young singer. It is necessary to have adequate space in the resonating cavities, but it also should be said that there have been fine, successful singers who have not possessed all the physical attributes usually thought to be desirable. Thus, emphasis should be placed on the use made of the physical attributes the student does possess.

MENTAL AND CULTURAL DEVELOPMENT

Since singers perform music with text, your ability to learn languages will be important. The text of the music studied is frequently drawn from a work of literature, and thus literature is one of the more important related areas to study. In many instances, it is possible to study a work of literature and later to find the same text in the music you sing. Opera, oratorio, art songs, and choral music all frequently have texts taken from standard literary works, and wise students will acquaint themselves as thoroughly as possible with the subject matter, since such depth of background study is almost always shown in the performance. This related study often

[2]Viktor Fuchs, *The Art of Singing and Voice Technique* (New York: London House & Maxwell, 1964), p. 10.

requires work outside the usual curriculum, and your training will be most thorough if you will take the time to study subjects in the liberal arts as well as in music.

Your education should be in three parts: (1) You should study vocal techniques and other subjects in the music curriculum; (2) you should study related subjects that will provide greater understanding of the text being sung; and (3) you should be exposed to cultural experiences on a high artistic level. Much of this book is devoted to the study of vocal techniques, but it should be emphasized that cultural experiences also can be of significant benefit. Although it is not necessary for a young person to come from a financially comfortable family that attends concerts regularly, exposure to good music at an early age can help to make progress more rapid.

If you have not yet been exposed to fine performances of music, it will be helpful for you to attend concerts and recitals of more experienced vocal and instrumental performers. Such musical exposure can give you some acquaintance with stage deportment, musical repertoire, and the level of musical performance ultimately expected of you. Although the study of musical and related subject matter is normally undertaken in a formal, academic atmosphere, attendance at musical performances can be a less formal part of your educational experience.

VOCAL TECHNIQUE

There is no substitute for having a good vocal instrument, but it is possible to teach the fundamentals of singing to almost anyone who is interested in learning. However, there can be a problem if too much emphasis is placed on any one technical process. There are many schools of thought, and no one should consider that any single school of thought has all the answers. For example, the Italian *bel canto*[3] is one of the most important historical periods in singing. But even bel canto cannot be expected to provide every singer with every answer to every situation. You should take information that works for you from any of several schools of thought, and you should use that information as a basis for improving your own singing. Do not try to imitate another singer; consume the information, perhaps modify it, and then make it a part of your own vocal technique.

THE PLACE OF VOCAL PRACTICE

The study of applied music always involves practice, but some aspects of applied music require more hours of practice than do others. Voice study, for example, may require less practice time than does piano study. But it is always important for you to give full attention to the music and the vocal techniques being practiced. It is the quality of your practice time that should be emphasized, and concentration is required if you are to utilize the practice period well. Any student who does not know what objective to work toward, or who has an attitude of "just going through exercises," will not progress.

Some teachers do not ask the student to spend any practice time outside the studio during the first few weeks, or months, of study. Their thinking is that the student does not yet have a sufficiently well developed concept of vocal technique, and therefore, the student cannot properly utilize practice time. If your concept of desirable technique or tone is not yet developed, independent vocal practice can be more of a problem than a help. It should be recognized that the practice period can be either good or bad; it all depends on whether you have a clear concept of the

---

[3]This term refers to the Italian vocal technique of the eighteenth century; its emphasis is on beautiful singing.

goal(s) to be achieved and whether you can concentrate on the work of the moment. When concentration is no longer possible, practice should stop, regardless of the length of time spent. It should also be noted that "students in college need to explore. It is hard to meld jazz and classical (legit) music. But if the proper balance is attained between the two, it shouldn't present a problem."[4]

In summary, a student will go a long way who already possesses a solid sense of musicianship, who possesses the natural physical characteristics appropriate for a singer, who has a capable mind, who has been exposed to cultural experiences, and who has a natural voice that will lend itself to good training. Many successful singers do not have all these attributes, but the five areas discussed in this unit give you an ideal standard by which to measure your own natural ability.

[4]"Sherrill Milnes: Baritone Extraordinare Talks About Vocal Jazz," interview by Gene Aitken, *Jazz Educators Journal,* 19, no. 1 (October-November 1986), 2.

2 *Choosing a Teacher*

It should be understood that a student of singing ordinarily studies with a teacher. But there are circumstances in which studying with a suitable teacher may not be possible. No one should assume that to study with just any teacher is always an asset. If an experienced, suitable teacher of singing is not available to you, you may need to proceed for a time on your own.

WHAT TO LOOK FOR IN A TEACHER

It may be difficult for you, as you begin your study, to find valid advice about your future as a singer. If so, you will need to assume more responsibility than another student who already can rely on an experienced teacher. But choosing your first teacher, or making a decision to work for a time by yourself, can be one of the most basic and important decisions you will make. It is not possible to give specific rules to be followed by every student, but there are guidelines that can be helpful to any beginning student of singing.

The American Academy of Teachers of Singing (membership in which is contingent on review by a national committee) believes that the teacher should possess the following attributes:[1]

A thorough general and musical education including sight-singing and ear training. He must be musically literate.

A substantial background in vocal study with competent teachers of singing over a period of at least five years. Each year should include a minimum of sixty hours of vocal and musical instruction.

A complete knowledge and understanding of the vocal instrument, including the basic features of its anatomy, how it functions, how to use it properly and effectively, and how to convey this knowledge clearly to the student.

Sensitivity to accuracy of intonation, quality of tone, and nuance of color.

A broad knowledge of vocal repertory, and styles of interpretation appropriate to opera, oratorio, art song, ballad, folk song, and musical theater.

Ability to classify a voice. (It is generally agreed that this important decision often needs to be delayed for some time. In an undeveloped voice there is a constant growth, if the teaching is correct. It is wiser to defer a final classification of a voice until sufficient training has unmistakably revealed it.)

A thorough knowledge and command of the English language; complete mastery of English diction in song—through correct articulation, enunciation, and pronunciation—a knowledge of at least three foreign languages (Italian, German, and French) encompassing basic grammar and good performance diction.

A basic understanding of psychology and its effective use in the teaching of singing, including a sympathetic, discerning, and analytical approach to both personal and professional problems of the student.

The ability to demonstrate with his own voice the correct principles of good tone production and interpretation. (It must be remembered that many successful and promi-

[1]Permission to publish was granted by Earl Rogers, Publications Officer of the American Academy of Teachers of Singing.

nent teachers have not been established vocal performers, and many noted singers have not achieved success as teachers.)
  Some competence at the piano.

In the final analysis, the teacher must have the ability, coupled with a compelling desire, to impart knowledge.

INDEPENDENT STUDY CAN BE HELPFUL

If it is not possible for you to locate a teacher who has the qualifications recommended by the American Academy of Teachers of Singing, you may be able to make progress in some areas by working independently. First, you must be able to read music. If you do not possess that ability already, then it will be possible for you to progress by learning to read music notation in one of the ways listed in Unit 1.

You also may be able to progress in working to improve your breath support. Instructions given in Units 5, 6, and 7 will provide the basic information. However, at some point, you will need to have an experienced, objective person give you an opinion about how you are progressing. Since breath support for the singer has many principles in common with breath support for those who play wind instruments, some help may be obtained by consulting a good teacher of clarinet, flute, or another wind instrument.

THE TAPE RECORDER

Many teachers of singing use a good tape recorder in the studio so that students can hear their own voices. Because hearing yourself, or feeling the sensations of resonance, is important if you are to progress, a tape recorder can be helpful, particularly if you have no qualified teacher to guide you.

If you use a tape recorder to hear yourself sing, it must be of fine quality. The equipment must be able to reproduce, without distortion, the sounds you actually sing; otherwise, you may believe you have a singing problem when the problem actually lies with the recorder.

SOME LIMITATIONS OF INDEPENDENT STUDY

It should be understood that independent study is to be undertaken only if a competent teacher is not available. Although a fine tape recorder can be useful, there is no real substitute for a competent, experienced teacher to listen to your singing and make suggestions for your improvement.

It is also important that an experienced teacher outline priorities during your first months of study. Most people can really concentrate on only one or two points at a time, and someone must make the decision about which aspects of the singing art you should concentrate on first. Written guidance is provided in this book, and advice sometimes can be obtained from teachers in related areas of study, but it is often the teacher of singing who can be most helpful. For your best results, the information contained in this book should be used along with the observation and advice of an experienced teacher of singing.

Just how you proceed in your study may not be entirely for you to say. You may not have a choice of teachers. Very often, a young student is assigned to a particular teacher who is thought by a third person to be "right" for that particular student. So there can be problems even under the best of circumstances. All you should expect to do is to pursue the most favorable circumstances available to you, work diligently, and then move toward more ideal circumstances later, after you have gained more experience.

You may feel you are almost alone in your attempt to become a mature, trained singer, but you should remember that many others have traveled that route before you. Although there are potential problems, the real problems are rarely so great that an eager, talented student cannot overcome them. It should be remembered most of all that "correct singing habits established during the school and college years will remain with the singer throughout adulthood. Many of our well-trained soloists and choristers continue their study of voice and sing with 'young' voices after they have reached the ages of fifty, sixty, or seventy."[2]

In conclusion, you should be aware that a student who has real interest and talent will improve. There are many ways to perfect your talent, and you cannot pattern your own progress after that of another person. If your circumstances are less than ideal, you should not be discouraged; if you seek the best advice available and if you persevere, you will have a good start toward becoming a mature singer. This book will make available to you information about the principles of singing. When those principles have been studied and made your own, you will have a solid basis for progress.

[2]Paul Peterson and others, "The Solo Voice and Choral Singing," *The Choral Journal,* XI, no. 4 (December 1970), 12. *Note:* This article was reprinted from *Internos* (April 1970), published only for members of the National Association of Teachers of Singing.

3 *Self–Consciousness*

Virtually every singer who performs in public has experienced self-consciousness at some time. A few singers may find self-consciousness to be only a very temporary situation, but many students have real difficulty in overcoming this problem. If you do not sing as freely and easily as you would like in front of an audience, you are to be counted among the majority of young singers.

It is necessary for each performer to work to minimize this problem. It is important for you not to let it inhibit your performance noticeably over a prolonged period of time. Experience will help you, and you can gain experience by accepting appropriate invitations to sing. For example, you may have an opportunity to sing for your class or chorus; you may have been asked to sing in a studio recital or a music department recital. The specific situation is less important than how you feel about approaching it. You may be quite comfortable when you sing for your teacher but self-conscious when you first sing for a larger, more diverse audience.

NERVOUSNESS

It should be understood that some nervousness can be an advantage to a performer. No singer, however experienced, will be at his best if he is not ''up'' for a particular performance—and being ''up'' involves some degree of anticipation or nervousness. A singer will learn through experience how to prepare mentally for a performance; that learning process may take only a short time, or it may take a year or more. However long it takes, it will be important for you to give continued attention to overcoming your own self-consciousness.

Nervousness, as the term is used here, can be thought of as being related to excitement, and excitement can almost always enhance your performance. A performance without any sense of excitement is often considered to be too routine, and routine singing will not get the best response from an audience. To describe a musical performance as exciting, sensitive, or imaginative is to recognize that the singer communicated well. This added, though perhaps nebulous, element should make any musical performance more interesting, and an excessively nervous singer cannot communicate genuine excitement and sensitivity.

You will sing best if you are able to shift your nervousness to a more positive attitude, but that can be such a problem that a particular singer may not be able to portray anything more than a sense of inadequacy. Audiences may have sympathy for young, inexperienced student singers, but their sympathy will ultimately turn to a lack of interest unless the singers learn how to use their own nervousness to strengthen their performance. Singers who let nervousness detract from their singing over a long period of time are actually too worried about what other people think of their performance; they are too self-centered at the moment of their public performance to communicate well.

It should be emphasized again that almost all young singers are nervous when performing for other people. It seems to be a common experience, but you will gradually be able to diminish this problem if you maintain a positive attitude over a period of time. You will be more comfortable as you gain experience, and you should always keep your long-term goal in mind. That goal is for you to be able to use the element of anticipation, or nervousness, before a performance to your own advantage, rather than to let it cause you a problem in communicating with your audience.

SHYNESS

It is necessary for a singer to remain "loose," to be emotionally and physically free while singing. If you are too shy or if you are preoccupied with the technique of singing, you will not be able to communicate well. No one should expect you to change overnight in your attempt to free yourself of shyness, but you should try to "let yourself go" more each time you sing. A friendly audience will understand, and an experienced teacher will know that you must try some of your own ideas before you can feel comfortable before an audience.

It is always necessary for a singer to project more broadly when singing for a large audience than for a small one. Serious students of singing will communicate out of a genuine desire to share their singing and music with other people, and singers with such a point of view will not need to worry about how they are being accepted. They will have broadened the center of attention to include the music and text.

FRIGHT

Fright is said to be fear excited by sudden danger, and a public performance can be viewed as a time of potential sudden danger. There are occasions when anyone can feel quite alone, and solo singing in public can be one of those occasions. It is not at all unusual for a singer to feel comfortable while practicing and singing in the studio but to feel uncomfortable while performing the same music for an audience. It is not as difficult for a choral singer; there is strength in numbers, and a member of a chorus almost never experiences fright to the same extent as a soloist. Any singer is most exposed when he or she performs individually.

Fright is a state of mind from which physical rigidity can result. It is the rigidity, or lack of physical flexibility, that causes the actual problem. The solution is first to try to change your state of mind. You should try to eliminate, or at least diminish, your feeling of fright by substituting a feeling of self-confidence. Fright, to a performer, is essentially self-consciousness, and it is never good for you to be too worried about how your performance is being received. The ideal, of course, is for you to be loose enough, and confident enough, to sing well but still not give the appearance of arrogance. You should try to move toward a state of communicating your art meaningfully.

You can approach fear by trying to focus your thinking away from yourself and toward the music and your audience. Some people advocate that you take several deep breaths before singing, and this exercise may help. Whatever your own favorite avenue for preparing to sing, it is important for you, first, to be able to maintain the same vocal habits you used previously in practice and, second, to focus your attention on making your audience understand and enjoy your music. People who feel fear often are also emotionally sensitive, and emotional sensitivity can be an important asset for any singer. Excitement can be contagious, and it can add an important dimension to your performance.

HOW TO OVERCOME SELF-CONSCIOUSNESS

It is not enough to recognize the symptoms of self-consciousness; if you are to solve this problem, you will need to have a specific plan.

1. *Be certain you are thoroughly prepared.* There is nothing that will help build confidence as much as knowing you are prepared. It is not possible to substitute inspiration of the moment for vocal and musical preparation. Each has its place, but inspiration and careful preparation are not interchangeable. You can be more self-confident when you know you are thoroughly prepared.

2. *Keep an optimistic attitude.* You will perform best when you are "loose," and you cannot maintain physical and mental looseness when you are worried. A positive attitude is the proper basis for correcting your problem, but it usually requires prolonged attention and work to overcome real self-consciousness.

3. *Recognize that self-consciousness exists only in your own thinking.* It is only a state of mind, and you will only prolong your problem if you insist on such negative thinking.

4. *Accept many opportunities to gain experience in singing for an audience.* There is no substitute for training and experience. It is important for you to sing sufficiently often that performance becomes a more usual situation for you, thus reducing your fear.

5. *Keep your attention on interpreting and communicating the music.* Self-consciousness is diminished by moving your attention away from yourself. If you will concentrate on your music and your audience, you will have little or no time for thinking about any self-consciousness you may feel.

6. *Take several deep breaths before you begin to sing.*[1] Fear may cause your usual breathing to be more shallow, which can be counteracted by taking several deep breaths. Fear tends to increase as the body receives less oxygen, so it is important to breathe deeply several times before you begin to sing or before you walk on stage.

Finally, it should now be recognized that self-consciousness is felt by most young singers. If you find that it persists, you should give your attention to the previous discussion, which will help to replace your feeling of self-consciousness with those more positive attitudes appropriate to a performer. When you can make the adjustments necessary, you will enjoy yourself more, and your singing will become more interesting.

[1]See Unit 5.

4 *Posture and Singing*

The objectives of this unit are to develop an understanding of good posture and to present physical exercises that will help you acquire it.

Good posture is a part of a singer's training that is often not given sufficient attention. It is a subject that can be easily understood, but good posture is not so often actually maintained while singing. You should know without question that your singing can be better if you cultivate better posture, and you should know that such improvement can be undertaken almost as independent study. Because this subject is closely related to the discussion of breath control, you should refer to Unit 5.

WHY GOOD POSTURE IS IMPORTANT

Every musician uses a musical instrument for performing, and a singer's instrument is his or her own body. You cannot change your physical makeup, but it is possible for you as a singer to benefit from better use of your body.

Since one of your major objectives is to sing with a free, resonant tone, it is important for you to create more ideal physical conditions for producing such a tone. You need to devote time and effort toward the improvement of your posture, and both mental involvement and physical balance are important factors.

CHARACTERISTICS OF GOOD POSTURE

Solo singers sing while standing, but many choruses rehearse while sitting. Thus, singers need to have information about both aspects of this subject.

Posture while Standing. It is recommended that you **stand as much as possible** while you sing, for good posture is easier to achieve while you are standing. You will have a better chance of realizing your full potential, for either choral or solo singing, if you will observe the recommendations given in this unit.

It is important for you to realize that most adults normally do not have good posture while singing. When you allow your body to remain in its usual position, the weight tends to be too heavy, or to push downward, and a downward force is not conducive to good singing. The **desired goal** is to maintain a physical balance, which can be realized if you observe the standards contained in the following ten points.

1. *You should stand "tall."* Such a physical position will have the effect of keeping your body "in line"; you will have a feeling of lifting from the diaphragm, which can give you a greater sense of security. According to one teacher, the student should have the sensation of being gently lifted from the back of the head as by a large rubber band. The feeling should be one of support.
2. *Your feet should be placed slightly apart.* Your toes should be pointed slightly outward, and one foot should be placed slightly forward of the other. You should have both feet

firmly in contact with the floor, and such a position should help to give you a feeling of greater confidence.

3. *Your weight should be centered slightly forward.* You should feel your weight being directed downward toward your feet. You should never feel "flat on your heels"; such a position is rigid and lacking in resilience. Nor should your weight be shifted too far forward; that, too, often will cause a feeling of insecurity. Again, the proper stance is with your weight centered slightly forward, your feet solidly in contact with the floor.

4. *Your knees should not feel locked or immobile.* Your knees should be relaxed and slightly bent. Then you have the possibility of moving more easily either backward or forward. Such movement ultimately will be natural for you, and it will help you to feel free and loose while you are singing.

5. *Your hips should be forward, and your weight should be evenly distributed.* The even distribution of your weight will help keep your spine straight, which will help in your total feeling of upward lift.

6. *Your spine should feel stretched upward,* and you should try to minimize any excessive curvature that may exist. Your back should be straight, and the feeling of lifting upward will help you to create the proper physical conditions for developing better breath support. Again, the proper feeling is one of lifting and gently stretching upward.

7. *Your chest should be held high; your shoulders should be back, free, and loose; your lower ribs should feel comfortably expanded; and your neck should be straight.* Essentially, this posture will let you feel expansion in the ribs and chest; the neck should be straight, and it should feel as if it is simply a continuation of your spine. There should not be a feeling of stretching in the front of your neck. Your chest should remain high at all times, and you should not let your chest cave in as your breath is used in singing.

8. *You should drop your arms easily and loosely at your sides.* Your arms should be slightly bent at the elbows. However, it is also quite acceptable to place one hand loosely in the other in front of your body and just above your waistline.

9. *Your head should be held high.* You should have the freedom to move your head easily from side to side, and you should direct your attention neither too high nor too low. You should not look at the floor, but neither should you hold your chin too high. As was suggested in point 1, you should have the feeling of lifting or of stretching as with a large rubber band.

10. *There should be no feeling of flabbiness.* Your body should have the feeling of total support and of being in line so you can physically support your sung tone. This feeling is one of being solidly in contact with the floor and of stretching from the spine upward.

These ten points are applicable to all singing. A basic part of your training is to learn these points so that you ultimately will make good posture automatically your own. You should also remember that posture and breathing are very closely related.

Posture while Sitting. Choral singers often rehearse while sitting, and the following points are directed primarily to them. Students in voice classes may either stand or sit, but it is recommended that they stand as much as is agreeable with the group. A solo singer normally sings while standing, and all singers normally stand while performing.

Instructions for a seated singer essentially duplicate, from the waist up, those instructions given to a singer who is standing. The real differences take place from the hips downward.

1. *Your feet should be placed on the floor as firmly as possible.* It is normal for one foot to be placed slightly in front of the other, and they should be somewhat apart.

2. *Your hips should be placed toward the back of the chair, and the weight of your body should be forward toward your feet.*

3. *Your back and shoulders should be inclined slightly forward, away from the back of the chair.*

4. *Your spine should have the feeling of being stretched upward.*

5. *Your chest should be held high and quiet; your shoulders should be back, free, and loose; your lower ribs should feel comfortably expanded; and your neck should be*

straight. Again, you should feel that your neck is simply a continuation of your spine. There should be no feeling of stretching in the front of your neck.

6. *You should drop your arms easily to your sides.* You may also place one hand loosely in the other, with both hands held in front of you and slightly above your waist. This is good posture unless, of course, you are holding music.

7. *Your head should be held high.* You should have the freedom to move your head easily from side to side, and you should gently tuck in your chin. You should not tilt your head backward, for that will stretch the front of the neck.

8. *There should be no feeling of flabbiness.* Your muscles should be in tune, for physical effort is required for you to adequately support a free, open tone.

The two chief points to remember are that your feet should be solidly in contact with the floor and that you should have a feeling of stretching upward from the spine. You should give your attention to those points first, and then you can move on to all aspects of refining your posture.

Physical Exercises

Standing

1. Stand tall; do not slump.

2. Raise your arms up to shoulder height, as in a gesture of appeal. Your arms are to be extended, but slightly bent, in front of your body and slightly to the side; then lower your arms slowly. This step should be practiced with the palms of your hands held upward.

3. Repeat the exercise as described in number 2, but now coordinate the movements with your breathing. Inhale while raising your arms, and exhale while lowering your arms. (You should also be careful to observe those instructions given for Posture while Standing.)

Seated

I

1. Lean forward from a sitting position, and place your forearms on your knees.

2. Slowly take a deep, full breath, and observe the expansion of the lower rib cage around your body. (You should also be careful to observe those instructions given for Posture while Seated.)

II

Sit to your greatest height; slowly take a deep, full breath, and observe the expansion of the lower rib cage around your body.

Finally, it should be emphasized that those exercises used to improve posture and those used to improve breath control are quite similar. In many instances, the same exercises can be used to improve in the two areas.

5 *Breath Control*

The objective of this unit is to develop an understanding of diaphragmatic-costal breathing and to clarify ways to develop more efficient breath control.

It is of primary importance for you to learn to make more efficient use of your breath, and there are several specific points to be learned before your breath can be well controlled. Units 5, 6, and 7 present a comprehensive approach for improving breath control. Among other points, you need to know how to breathe, problems related to inhaling too little or too much breath, exercises to help improve your breath control, and how to conserve your breath.

PREVIOUS EXPERIENCE

Breath control is not new to any singer; it is only a matter of changing and refining existing habits—although it is never easy to change a habit. It has been said that a small child naturally breathes correctly, but the child often learns less efficient habits while growing up.[1] Any person who has played a wind instrument, or who has engaged in another activity where the use of breath is important, may already have developed relatively refined habits of breath support. But anyone can work to improve present habits, and the following pages contain information that will show you how to proceed.

THE BASIS OF SINGING

One of the most basic steps in singing is to learn how to control your breath. Although proper breath support does not in itself assure beautiful singing, mastery of the techniques included here can serve as a solid foundation on which to build your voice. More efficient support with your breath can improve your singing within a relatively short period of time. But careful attention to breath support is a continuing requirement of all singers, no matter how accomplished they may already have become.

It should not be difficult for you to understand how the tone should be supported with the breath, but making the most effective use of your knowledge may become a lesson in self-discipline. It almost always requires perseverance to change a habit, and the following points should receive your daily attention. This aspect of voice study should not require long sessions with a teacher, but your own careful and continuous attention under supervision will be most productive.

---

[1]Changes in the skeleton that occur after a child begins to walk actually preclude maintenance of the exact breathing technique used by an infant.

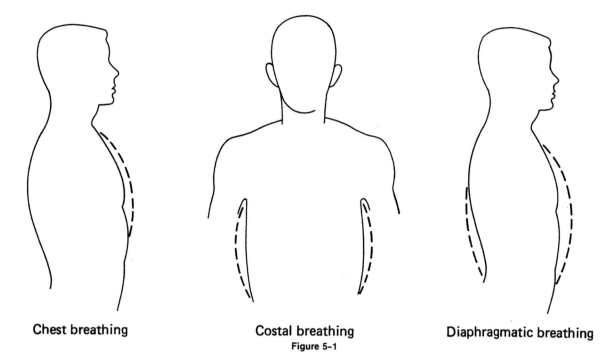

Chest breathing   Costal breathing   Diaphragmatic breathing

Figure 5-1

TYPES OF BREATH CONTROL

Posture is important to good breath support, and the information contained in Unit 4 should be reviewed before you proceed. The three usual types of breathing are shown in Figure 5-1. Chest (clavicular) breathing is not recommended for use in singing; it does not provide adequate breath support. A combination of rib (costal) and diaphragmatic (abdominal) breathing does serve very well and is therefore recommended.

Chest, or Clavicular, Breathing.   Many beginning singers learn to breathe from the chest before starting voice study. Chest breathing will not give you a sufficient physical foundation for supporting your tone, and this discussion is included here so you can understand its basic limitations.

"This is the kind of breathing used by the exhausted athlete, the person who is 'out of breath.' It is 'last resort,' desperate breathing."[2] The heaving chest is the most obvious physical characteristic of chest breathing, which does not utilize the full capacity of your lungs.

You should avoid any real movement of your chest and shoulders. To focus your breathing in those areas is to provide insufficient control over exhalation. When your chest is collapsed after the singing of a musical phrase, your shoulders drop, and your physical posture is almost certain to be poor. Such a position does not allow proper breath support. Also, you would again bring your chest and shoulders into an erect position with the taking of your next breath. Repetition of this process takes more energy than you should use, it does not provide enough support for producing your best sound, and it looks awkward. Further, breathing from your chest and shoulders, with its usual lack of support, can lead to unnecessary tension. Such breathing often creates tension in the neck, and it can easily spread until the

[2]William Vennard, *Singing: The Mechanism and the Technic* (New York: Carl Fischer, Inc., 1967), p. 27.

"upper portion of the anatomy becomes rigidly inflexible. Continued use of clavicular breathing leads to tonal 'throatiness.'"[3]

You should have the habit of raising your chest easily, but not excessively; letting your shoulders relax; and letting your arms hang loosely. Such posture will let you breathe by expanding and contracting your diaphragm. If your chest is collapsed, your abdominal muscles will not be able to work as effectively, and you will have trouble supporting your tone with your breath.

Breathing from your upper chest may seem most natural to you because it may already have become automatic. But changing this habit should be the goal of every student from the very beginning. Your ultimate objective should be to inhale through your nose and mouth. When you take such a breath, the air moves down and causes your body to expand. Without the expansion of your body, there will not be sufficient support.

Diaphragmatic-Costal Breathing.   The combination of these two types of breathing will make it possible for you to support your tone adequately.

Costal (rib) breathing may be observed by the outward expansion of your ribs. You may determine how well you are using costal breathing by following these simple steps: (1) Place your hands over the front portion of your lower ribs (with the palms of your hands toward your body); (2) move your hands forward until the tips of your fingers touch when your breath has been exhaled; (3) inhale a full breath to move your hands as far apart as possible. If these steps are performed with your breath, and not by simply moving your hands, they will help you take a full, deep breath.

These steps also may be performed by placing your hands at the small of your back, but it is possible to expand your body much less when this position is used. It will be easiest to feel this expansion when working in the front, although it is possible to check for physical expansion either way.

These steps are vitally important, but they represent only one aspect of the total process of learning to breathe properly. You should coordinate them with the following information.

Diaphragmatic (abdominal) breathing is often described simply as "using the diaphragm." But recent research indicates that the diaphragm is most central when you inhale; costal (rib) and epigastrium (located just below the breast bone) muscles are important in controlling your tone as you sing the musical phrase.[4]

The diaphragm is usually described as the muscle that separates the abdominal cavity from the chest cavity. It is, perhaps, the most powerful muscle in your body, and its proper use is of primary importance for proper breath support. When you inhale, the diaphragm flattens, which has the effect of lowering the floor of your chest. (See Figure 5–2.) "It should be the goal of the singer and student to preserve, habitually, the open rib cage in order that the diaphragm will remain in its low position. This will cause the lungs to fill,"[5] and the breath capacity can be maintained. It is this control, then (brought about through good posture, the open rib cage, and the lowered diaphragm), that makes possible the best physical circumstances for supporting your sung tone.

[3]Cornelius L. Reid, *The Free Voice: A Guide to Natural Singing* (New York: Coleman-Ross Company, Inc., 1965), p. 161.

[4]Van A. Christy, *Foundations in Singing,* 4th ed. (Dubuque, Iowa: Wm. C. Brown, 1979), p. 25.

[5]Dale V. Gilliland, *Guidance in Voice Education* (Columbus: Ohio State University School of Music, 1970), p. 23.

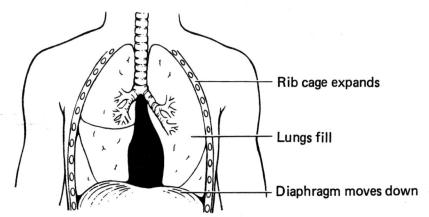

Figure 5-2 Diaphragmatic-Costal Breathing. *Ivan Trusler, Walter Ehret*, Functional Lessons in Singing, *2nd ed., © 1972, p. 3. Reprinted by permission of Prentice-Hall, Inc., Englewood Cliffs, N.J.*

WHAT TO DO

Stated in a brief, direct manner, the proper physical conditions for breathing are as follows:

1. Maintain a comfortably raised chest.
2. Keep the shoulders and arms loose and free from rigidity.
3. Keep the head in a natural, vertical position.
4. Maintain an open rib cage for maximum ease in lowering the diaphragm.
5. Maintain a resistance of the diaphragm to the upward lift in the abdominal region.
6. Maintain flexibility at the base of the rib cage.
7. Use both the mouth and the nose for inhaling. (This is of particular importance when taking a "catch" breath.)

These points are related to, and to some extent depend on, the physical posture you maintain, a subject discussed in greater detail in Unit 4. Your ultimate goal is to coordinate correct posture, proper breath support, and efficient use of the breath so that their proper execution becomes almost automatic. If you are a serious student of singing, you will check your mastery of these points at regular intervals!

WHAT TO AVOID

There are two points you should guard against when you take a breath.

1. When your diaphragm has lowered, it presses down against the stomach and other organs. But those organs cannot be moved downward, which is one major reason many singers cannot perform well after having just finished a large meal. Those people do not have enough room for the food and a full breath of air. Of course, there are exceptions, but eating a full meal just before singing is not a good practice for most choral or solo singers.

2. You should avoid a stiff and rigid posture such as is most commonly associated with a soldier. Such a traditional posture stiffly raises the chest and pulls in the abdomen so hard that it cannot move sufficiently to aid in proper support. This position causes the same problem as eating just before singing. The organs are pushed against the diaphragm, and the singer cannot take a deep breath. "So when the singer exhales, there is nothing for him to do but drop his chest. When he inhales again, he once more hauls up his chest and shoulders. What he should be doing is

the exact opposite. The shoulders and chest should remain motionless, and the diaphragm and abdomen should move."[6]

THE POINT OF SUSPENSION

The point of suspension is a balance of air pressure created by those muscles involved with inhaling and opposed by those muscles involved with exhaling. You should not take a breath and then immediately begin to sing; there should be a brief moment of suspension between the time your breath is inhaled and actual singing begins.[7] Finding and maintaining this point of suspension is important to good, basic, free tone production. "The Italians . . . attempted to establish this sensation as a basic sensation for all singing. The wise singer will always use the point of suspension as a reference for correctly produced vocal sound."[8]

Physical Exercises

Before the actual physical exercises are listed, it will be well to discuss their purpose. Keep in mind that exercises are intended to help you produce a better tone; they should not be considered as an end in themselves. As soon as possible, you should coordinate the exercises with actual singing. The physical exercises will most often be helpful when used in singing short musical examples, and these exercises should never be discarded.

The five following physical exercises supply specific and logical steps for achieving improved breath control.

I

1. Inhale slowly, to the count of five.

2. Hold the breath (with no tightening in the throat or jaw) while counting to ten.

3. Exhale slowly, to the count of five.

You can improvise variations on the foregoing three stages; for example, the number of counts may be increased as you become more experienced. Begin with the number that presents a modest challenge; as your efficiency increases, lengthen the time allowed to inhale, hold, and exhale. This exercise should be used regularly and for short periods of time. As the steps become more controlled, you should practice the exercises while you sing a vowel sound on a comfortable pitch. Begin with the most natural sound (usually an *uh, ah,* or *ee*), and leave the less natural sounds until a later time.

II

1. Inhale quickly.

2. Exhale slowly. Spin out the breath through partially closed lips. It may help to verbalize an *s,* or a hissing sound.

The foregoing exercise is sometimes described as being the equivalent of taking a "surprise breath." Because the exercise creates a situation quite close to the use of your breath in actual singing, you will often find that its use contributes to better control.

---

[6]Vennard, *Singing,* p. 29.

[7]Any tendency to close the throat can detract from the value of this point.

[8]Ralph D. Appleman, *The Science of Vocal Pedagogy* (Bloomington: Indiana University Press, 1967), p. 11.

III

1. Stand tall; do not slump.

2. Raise your arms up to shoulder height, as in a gesture of appeal. Extend your arms, slightly bent, in front of your body and slightly to your side; then lower your arms slowly. Practice this step with the palms of your hands held upward.

3. Repeat the exercise described in number 2, but now coordinate the movements with your breathing. (Inhale while raising your arms, and exhale while lowering your arms.) You should keep your chest comfortably raised, your rib cage open, and the base of your rib cage flexible. Keep your lips parted, and take your breath primarily through your mouth.

IV

1. Lean forward from a sitting position, and place your forearms on your knees.

2. Slowly take a deep, full breath, and observe the expansion of your lower rib cage around your body.

V

1. Sit tall, with your back straight and your chest comfortably high.

2. Slowly take a deep, full breath, and observe the expansion of the lower rib cage around your body.

Musical Exercises

You should first sing the following exercises with a moderately full tone, but with no sensation of singing unusually loudly or softly. The objective is to begin to co-ordinate the support of your breath in music, and the use of a moderately full tone will serve that purpose best. Since voices differ in size, no specific dynamic marking is recommended, but your sound should always be easily and freely produced.

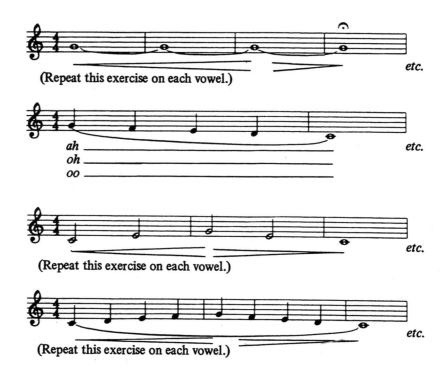

(Repeat this exercise on each vowel.)

(Repeat this exercise on each vowel.)

(Repeat this exercise on each vowel.)

The foregoing exercises are some of the most natural for singers. The exact range can be transposed, and you should find your most comfortable range. After that optimum range has been determined, you should transpose the exercise down by half-steps until you are no longer comfortable, and then move up by half-steps until you are no longer comfortable with the high notes. This step will help you to find your full, functional range.

The primary vowels used in singing are sounded as follows: (1) *ah* as in *father,* (2) *eh* as in *feather,* (3) *ee* as in *feet,* (4) *o* as in *oh,* and (5) *u (oo)* as in *too.* Although all mouth shapes are individual, certain of these vowels are generally better for the beginning singer to use. The mouth shape will normally be most natural for *ah, oh,* and *ee,* and it is recommended that you use those vowels first. However, you should know that some teachers like to use the *uh* sound.

The following exercises may be sung in unison or in octaves.

The foregoing exercises are designed to

1. Help improve your technique of taking a breath and make the use of your breath more efficient.

2. Begin to give you a concept of a vocal line.
3. Help you get the "feel" of vowels by using them in a variety of situations. (Remember, these exercises are to be moved downward and then upward in pitch; in that way you will exercise your usual range.)

The exercises have been written on a single pitch or have been limited to a range of just five tones. At some point you will be ready to move to exercises that utilize a full octave. The following vocal exercises will build on what has just been presented, but you should not practice them if there is any noticeable question about your singing of the previous exercises. Also, you should stop practicing the exercises that follow if, after several repetitions, there is not a full, free tone throughout the octave. In such a situation, it will be best for you to wait until a voice teacher can supervise your singing.

(Repeat this exercise on each vowel.)

(Repeat this exercise on each vowel.)

There are generally accepted practices to be observed when taking a breath in singing. It should be emphasized again that the use of these exercises is fundamental to the development of optimum breath support. But the ultimate goal is to put these techniques to use in music. The repertoire included in the last part of this book is chosen to help you implement techniques already learned.

In singing,

1. Do not breathe within a phrase or clause.
2. Do not breathe between or within syllables of the same word.
3. Take time for a breath (where there is no rest) from the last note of a phrase; do not take time from the first note of the next musical phrase.
4. Do not let the taking of a breath interrupt the rhythmic flow of the music.

The accepted musical practice of using an apostrophe (') as a breath mark will be followed here. The apostrophe within a circle (⊙) indicates that taking a breath is optional (see the first apostrophe in the following example); the apostrophe alone indicates that a breath is normally to be taken (see the second apostrophe). The following musical example was taken from ''Down by the Sally Gardens,'' arranged by T. C. Kelly.

MUSIC FOR PRACTICE[9]

All through the Night
Who Is Sylvia? (An Sylvia)

[9]To locate pieces in this book, refer to the listing on pages vi and vii.

6 *The Catch Breath*

Units 4 and 5 were devoted to a discussion of proper posture and breath support, and you are encouraged to review that material. It is necessary to understand those subjects before you begin to work on the catch breath. A catch breath must be taken more rapidly, when no time is provided in the music for a usual, longer breath.

Most people ordinarily breathe through their noses, but in taking a catch breath you will be obliged to inhale more rapidly. Thus, you should learn to inhale through your mouth and nose, because sufficient air cannot be taken through your nose alone. Because too much air taken through your mouth may tend to dry out your throat, you should inhale as much air as possible through your nose and some through your mouth.

The steps for taking a catch breath are the same as those for taking an ordinary breath: Inhale, suspend the breath, sing, and exhale. The difference is that a catch breath must be inhaled much more rapidly. You should begin to practice the four steps slowly and then increase your speed as you become more proficient. You may want to approach the catch breath as simply taking a normal breath more quickly.

Although there will be situations in which it will be advisable for you to work with your teacher to perfect your catch breath, it is also possible for you to work on the basic steps during your own practice time.

USE OF THE CATCH BREATH

Sometimes you will not have enough time to take a breath for singing the next musical phrase. At some time every singer must take a breath in the shortest possible time. Some choral singers stagger their breathing because they have not yet refined their breathing to a point where they can effectively sing a really long musical phrase in one breath, or perhaps the conductor wishes to achieve a continuous musical texture. Of course, a solo singer has no one else with whom to cooperate in staggered breathing. It will be well for you now to focus your attention on the technique of taking a catch breath so your breathing may successfully serve the music you sing.

There should be no problem at all in taking an adequate breath where there is a rest of some length in the music. But a catch breath is taken where no time is provided; it is then necessary for you to recognize where in the music to take the breath and to be able to take an adequate breath in the shortest possible time.

It should be obvious that the musical phrase should not be noticeably interrupted. The melodic line ordinarily builds toward a climactic point and then moves away from that point, and to interrupt such inherent musical motion would tend to compromise your ability to interpret adequately what the composer has written. Learning how to take a catch breath will allow your technique to be under your control, and the mechanics of your singing will not detract from the music. Thus, your own attention and the attention of your audience can properly be focused on your interpretation of the music.

The following musical example is taken from an English folk song, "The Turtle Dove," and each breath mark shows where a singer must take a catch breath.

Because such instances are seen quite regularly, the solo singer has no choice other than to learn how to negotiate long phrases smoothly and musically.

In this example, and in every other instance where a catch breath is required, you should breathe by taking time away from the note preceding the breath mark. You should never be late in starting the note following the breath mark.

Any teacher who has worked with young singers for any length of time knows that a common problem is the student's use of shallow breathing; such a lack of breath support tends to tighten the throat. Tension in the throat diminishes the possibility of resonance, and the student's vocal tone is automatically less full. The tone may even be distorted.

The desired goal is to achieve a spontaneous release as a result of the diaphragmatic impulse. A feeling of supporting the sung tone from the diaphragm tends to free the throat and increase the possibility of resonance. The sound will be freer, and any singer should have greater vocal vitality. Such circumstances are always desirable, but it is probable that you will find them more difficult to achieve when you are taking a catch breath because of the limitation of time.

Physical Exercises ───

Since a catch breath is always taken quickly, the following exercises should be practiced quickly. There are additional exercises in Units 5 and 7 that may also be helpful. The emphasis now is on taking a good, deep breath; taking the breath quickly; and starting the tone.

I

1. Place the tips of the fingers of one hand one or two inches below your breastbone.

2. Use your mouth and nose to inhale a full breath as quickly as possible. You should take most of the air through your nose, but take some air through your mouth also.

II

1. Practice the preceding two steps, but now add the following.

2. With a full, energetic sound, sing (or speak) *hah* or *hoh* several times. Focus your attention on the physical action as felt by your fingertips. The development of this normal action of the diaphragm represents a most basic step toward producing a quick, correct support of the sung tone. This exercise may be spoken, sung on a medium pitch, or sung with detached tones on a one-three-five-three-one arpeggio.

III

1. Inhale quickly through your nose and mouth.

2. Exhale slowly. Spin out your breath through partially closed lips. It may help to verbalize an *s,* or a hissing sound.

IV

1. Lean forward from a sitting position, and place your forearms on your knees.

2. Quickly take a deep, full breath, and observe the expansion of your lower rib cage around your body.

V

1. Sit tall, with your back straight and your chest comfortably high, and repeat the preceding exercise.

2. Quickly take a deep, full breath, and observe the expansion of the lower rib cage around your body.

Musical Exercises

You should first sing the following exercises with a moderately full sound. The objective is to coordinate the catch breath with the sung tone. In every exercise, you should focus your attention first on taking your breath. The pitch given is only a representative example; you should choose a comfortable range for your own voice. Also, you should take a catch breath after each repetition of the exercise.

As was discussed in Unit 5, the primary vowels used in singing are *ah* as in *father, eh* as in *feather, ee* as in *feet, o* as in *oh,* and *u (oo)* as in *too.* First practice the preceding exercises with those vowels; after one or two vowel sounds have become quite comfortable, practice the ones remaining. Of course, ultimately you should have control of all vowel sounds after you have taken a catch breath.

It may be necessary for you to review the information contained in Units 5 and 6 several times before you feel you are really capable of utilizing the breath to your fullest advantage.

MUSIC FOR PRACTICE

Down by the Sally Gardens
Love Has Eyes

7 Breath Control: Starting and Stopping the Tone

The objective of this unit is to learn the proper way to start a vocal tone (attack), control the breath, and stop the tone (release). The physical exercises and musical examples are designed to help you learn how to produce a free, supported vocal tone.

Not only is it necessary for you to become more efficient in the technique of taking a breath, but it is equally important for you to be able to control the use of your breath while you are singing. Remember that a singer can inhale too much air; to do so is just as much a problem as to not take in enough! Techniques discussed in Units 5 and 6 can serve as the basis for more efficient breath control, and you should study those techniques again. But the breath must also be controlled after you have inhaled. Also, it is necessary for you to give particular attention to the starting and stopping of your sung tone.

It is true that certain muscles in the throat are used in singing; but because their use is involuntary, you should not be concerned about manipulating them. If your breath is taken properly, your muscles will have a greater tendency to work in harmony with the breath, and those muscles will be more relaxed. In this discussion, the recommended relaxed condition is to be thought of as an absence of tightness; there is no thought of complete looseness.

PREPARATION FOR SINGING

Mental preparation before the attack is to be emphasized, but many teachers and singers believe it is the ear that monitors the singing process. Both the ear and the mind are involved, of course. For example, "scooping" may occur because the singer has not prepared mentally, but it is the ear that makes the singer aware of producing a "good" or a "bad" sound.

It is important for you to have a feeling of freedom when the tonal attack is properly initiated, and there are steps that will help you achieve such refinement. The breathing of the average person consists simply of taking a breath and exhaling it. But the singer needs to observe the four following steps in all singing. At first you may need to be conscious of each step taken, but the sequence should ultimately become automatic.

I—Inhale;   II—Suspend the breath;   III—Sing;   IV—Exhale

This sequence should be followed each time a breath is taken. Of course, the music itself will dictate how much time is allowed for each step. For that reason, you should practice the sequence in all possible degrees between fast and slow.

STARTING THE TONE: THE ATTACK

You should look upon the attack as a completely usual part of your singing, but you should also understand what is involved in starting your sung tone. First, it is important that you use your breath efficiently; also, you should start your sung tone exactly on pitch. There should be no scooping up to a pitch, and there should be no excessive expulsion of your breath.

Incorrect Attacks. Two common mistakes are breathy and glottal attacks. A breathy attack occurs when the breath is applied before the vocal bands are ready. That is, the singer begins to sing without an efficient use of the breath.

A glottal attack occurs when the vocal bands close following the taking of the breath. The vocal bands then are not prepared for singing, and the result too often is an unpleasant "shock of the glottis." This attack is often called a throaty attack, and the remedy is to keep the vocal bands open after the breath is inhaled. When the glottal attack is a problem, the singer should think of forming the vowel higher in the throat (in the pharynx). The attention of the singer should be called away from the throat itself, and it may be helpful to start the tone above the main pitch to be sung, for example

Recommended Attack. Before the attack, there should be a clear concept of the vowel and pitch to be sung, and the vocal bands should be opened with a deep, full breath. The action of the breath and the vocal bands should be synchronized, achieving a balance. The proper adjustment must take place at once, and a singer who has made these adjustments correctly is said to have made a good attack.[1]

The action of the vocal bands is automatic. When a person breathes and does not speak or sing, the vocal bands relax and there is a wide space between them for the air. When the person is about to speak or sing, the edges of the vocal bands are brought closer together; they "form a narrow slit, through which the air rushes, setting the membranes in vibration and producing sound. And that is the act of phonation."[2]

Again, the proper approach is to concentrate on taking a breath. You should create the conditions for letting the vocal bands do their own work freely. They will work automatically, and you may only cause problems if you give them your close attention.

There are two types of attacks, staccato and legato. *Staccato singing* is usually thought to involve equal portions of sound and silence, an eighth note followed by an eighth rest, or a sixteenth note followed by a sixteenth rest, and so on. The breath moves suddenly in the staccato attack, for the notes are short. The attack should be light; each tone should be started sharply and stopped immediately. "There must never be a gutteral 'shock of the glottis' often heard. This cannot occur if the vocal bands are not closed after inhalation preceding the attack."[3]

---

[1]Some teachers also advocate what has been called the *imaginary H*—that is, an attack in which the breath slightly precedes the muscular closure of the vocal bands, letting the Bernoulli Effect precipitate the closure of the glottis.

[2]W. J. Henderson, *The Art of Singing* (New York: Dial Press, 1968), p. 38.

[3]Van A. Christy, *Expressive Singing*, 3rd ed., Vol. I (Dubuque, Iowa: Wm. C. Brown, 1974), p. 56.

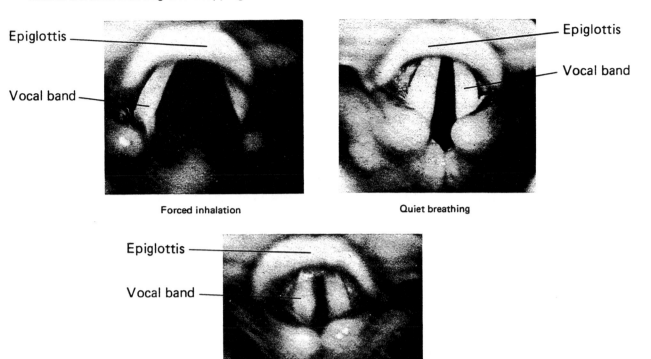

Forced inhalation Quiet breathing

Normal phonation

Figure 7-1 *Willard R. Zemlin*, Speech and Hearing Science: Anatomy and Physiology, *2nd ed. © 1981, p. 150. Reprinted by permission of Prentice-Hall, Inc., Englewood Cliffs, N.J.*

Many choral directors and some studio voice teachers ask the student to use an aspirate *h* to help "open" the throat and minimize the chance of a guttural attack. Although this device may be helpful in a chorus rehearsal, it is less useful in the voice studio, and its use is not recommended when the student is practicing alone. A better way to handle the staccato attack is to have a breath impulse for each note (but not a new breath), think of renewing the vowel sound for each new note, and release each note immediately and cleanly.

Legato singing is the type most often required. Only one beginning of the sung tone is required, as well as only one conclusion of the sung tone in each musical phrase; between the beginning and the concluding tones there is a long note, or a series of continuous notes. "Two important technics [*sic*] to master are the checking of breath in the 'open throat' following inhalation to establish breath suspension, and the quiet, precise attack of tone without loss of breath."[4] Some teachers ask their students to begin the tone with a hum, approximating the sound of an *n*. This technique may have its place, but such a tone must be well supported and freely produced.

The student should practice the vowel sounds, beginning with *uh, ee, oh,* and *ah,* in a manner similar to the practice of the staccato attack; the chief difference is that the legato tone continues throughout the total musical phrase without interruption. Singing a legato phrase has a different "feel" because the tone must be "carried" from one vowel sound, word, or note to another.

Finally, a common fault of young singers is to breathe from the chest; this

[4]Ibid., pp. 54-55.

lack of breath support almost always produces tightness in the throat. An attack that produces tension in the throat will not help to develop a full, resonant sound; under such conditions the sound will be distorted. A spontaneous freedom in singing is brought about by the use of diaphragmatic-costal breathing, which occurs when a balance of breath support has been achieved. It is most important to make the attack with a free, supported tone, and the following exercises are designed to help achieve such a balance.

Physical Exercises

I

1. Place the tips of the fingers of one hand one to two inches below your breast-bone.

2. With a full, energetic sound, say *hah* several times. Focus your attention on the action that takes place at your fingertips. Strengthening this normal action of the diaphragm in speaking is a most important step toward producing a proper attack of the sung tone.

II

1. With the tips of the fingers of one hand on the diaphragm, place your other hand on the abdominal wall.

2. Your jaw should hang loosely, and your tongue and lips should remain relaxed. While in such a relaxed position, sing *hah* with a full, short sound. This exercise may be repeated on a medium pitch, or it may be sung detached on a one-three-five-three-one arpeggio.

III

Sing the vowel sounds on repeated, short notes. Use a full sound, but strive to sing a pure vowel rather than push your breath toward a forced sound.

ee   ee   ee   ee   ee
(Repeat this exercise on *ah*, *oh*, and *oo*.)

CONTROLLING THE BREATH

The well-produced voice will always have breath in reserve even after having sung a long musical phrase. You must understand what is involved in taking a proper breath and be able to attack the tone cleanly. But those techniques may be highly developed and you may still not be able to control your breath while actually singing.

Your greatest problem in controlling your breath may be that you waste too much breath. A tendency of the inexperienced singer is to expel more breath than is needed when singing the first few notes of a musical phrase. It is inefficient to use so much breath on the first tones. The proper use is to maintain an even flow of breath throughout the musical phrase and still have breath left after the last note has been sung.

You should know how long you will be required to control your breath. It is not desirable to be stingy with your breath, for not to let your breath flow from the beginning to the end of the phrase will often bring on unnecessary tension in your voice. The physical response most appropriate is to preserve sufficient breath for the last note of the phrase, but also to "meter out" sufficient breath as the music progresses so you always have a legitimate physical feeling of motion. To try to save too much breath is to withdraw the very energy the vocal tone requires for maintaining its efficiency and vibrancy. It takes much practice for any student to find the exact "feeling" that will serve best.

STOPPING THE TONE: THE RELEASE

The release of a tone is an important part of singing, and too often it is not given the attention it deserves. In order to sing the last note of a musical phrase with a full, vibrant sound, you must have taken several steps in preparation for the final release.

1. You must know how long a musical phrase is to be sung before you attack the first note of the phrase.
2. You should know where the musical *high point* of the phrase is located. This term does not refer to pitch but to the musical focus of the phrase. The phrase normally moves toward the climactic point, and then it moves away from that point toward the release of the final tone.
3. Your initial attack should have been made cleanly and with a well-supported breath.
4. Your tone should be controlled throughout the musical phrase.
5. The last tone of a musical phrase should be "finished." To finish the final tone is to have prepared for the final release. That release must never be a surprise to the singer, and it should not appear to be a surprise to the listener.

If you implement these steps, you will always be prepared for each new note. There should be no surprises in singing a music composition that has been prepared for performance. Of course, these steps will be perfected as you study and rehearse the music, whether you are a soloist or a choral singer. The only difference is that an individual singer can work on any specific point that appears to need attention, whereas the choral singer must work as one member of the group. Thus, the choral director will decide which aspects of breath control and singing the chorus as a whole will rehearse.

The following exercises may also be sung in octaves.

Musical Exercises

I—Starting the Tone

(Repeat this exercise on *ah*, *oo*, and *ee*.)

ah ___   ah ___   ah ___   ah ___   ah ___ etc.
(Repeat this exercise on each vowel.)

mah   moh   meh   mee   moo   ah   oh   eh   ee   oo   etc.

II—Controlling the Breath and the Release

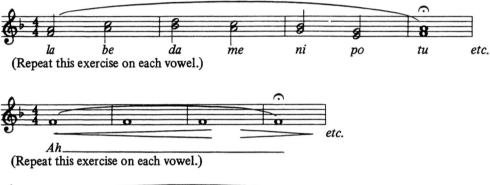

la   be   da   me   ni   po   tu   etc.
(Repeat this exercise on each vowel.)

Ah _____   etc.
(Repeat this exercise on each vowel.)

uh _____   oh ___   uh _____   etc.

The purpose of these exercises is better control of the breath and the release. The tempo and the pitch should be varied according to your particular needs, but the written pitches represent an approximate starting point for most voices. When transposing, it is recommended that the exercises first be moved down by half-steps and only later be moved higher than the written pitch. The actual range used should be limited to the vocal range in which you feel comfortable. Any exercise utilizing long notes should crescendo to a particular point and then decrescendo toward the release of the final tone.

MUSIC FOR PRACTICE

Greensleeves
Ah, Dearest Love (Caro mio ben)

8 *Singing*

with a Free Tone

After you have begun to support your breath from the diaphragm, your next major objective should be to sing with a free tone. A more refined and beautiful tone will tend to develop as your tone production becomes increasingly free. Your proper objective is to sing with a free tone, rather than to try immediately to produce a beautiful tone.

To make the production of a beautiful tone your first objective is to put your primary emphasis in the wrong place. Too often, it will result in trying to sing with tension and an unnatural sound, and such a lack of freedom will not allow you to refine your singing enough as you continue your study. Your tone can become increasingly free if you will have a concept of "singing on the breath";[1] as you achieve increased freedom in singing, you will be better able to communicate what you wish to express. That is, with a freer tone production you will not be so limited in the variety of tone color you can use; a freer tone production is much more flexible and trainable, and it will allow you ultimately to sing with emotional and intellectual sensitivity and musical perception.

Although you will properly give your attention first to refining your breath control, you should now build on that increased control by singing with a freer tone. You will need to achieve more refinement in both areas if you are ultimately to sing your best.

JUDGING YOUR OWN SINGING

It is always difficult for young singers to be able to judge their own singing; it may even be difficult for you to receive objective advice from another person.

The best advice about your singing will come from an experienced and successful teacher, but the use of a good tape recorder can also help you know something of how you sound. However, a tape recorder should not be viewed as a total answer in itself, and if you do use one, it is important to use a tape system with good fidelity.

RELAXATION

You cannot produce a free, resonant tone if you are tense. Your ability to sing while relaxed is of great importance to you, but you should first understand that for you to feel relaxed does not mean you should feel flabby or undisciplined. Relaxation for a singer is normally interpreted as a lack of rigidity or tension. No one should

[1]Good breath support.

really expect to sing well while feeling rigid or tense, for the muscles will be set in a particular position that allows little or no flexibility.

FEELING AND TONE PRODUCTION

Although you will ultimately want to become acquainted with the many physical aspects that influence resonance and tone production, the emphasis in your study should be on understanding the principles of good tone production and applying them. The teaching of singing is not generally regarded as a science. It would be misleading to list an exact set of steps for every student to follow, but it would be just as misleading to believe that there are no commonly accepted principles to use. The differences of opinion that sometimes exist among teachers are more directly related to the methods used in teaching; there is considerable agreement about the principles, or objectives, involved in building a mature vocal tone. For example, there is general agreement that vocal tone is greatly influenced by the vocal bands (they are the actuators of tone) and the use made of the resonance cavities.

Your basic sound is produced when the breath passes the vocal bands, which function automatically. Thus, you will achieve no good purpose if you try to analyze the working of your vocal bands while you are singing. Any conscious attempt to control the action of your vocal bands will only lead to constriction of your throat muscles, which will cause you to sing less freely. You will have achieved the best conditions for building your vocal tone when your throat feels free and open; if you have tightness or strain in your throat, you may be sure there is some problem.

The resonance cavities are the areas where your sound can be molded, and your attention to resonance and placement can make a real difference in how you sound, leading to further refinement of your sung tone. This refinement will be necessary if you are to progress toward a more mature use of your voice.

THE RESONATORS

The teaching of singing may be less tangible than the teaching of a musical instrument. An instrument has valves or keys; the teacher can see how well the students use those valves or keys; and the students can immediately know they are or are not pressing the correct finger(s). This aspect of the singing process is much less tangible, and it is often necessary to work indirectly when teaching a singer. But the central point here is to understand that the resonators can enhance the sound of any young singer. As Vennard says, "the frequency or pitch of a vocal tone is determined primarily by the vibrator, and usually only the timbre is modified by the resonators."[2]

That statement gives some information about the functions of the vocal bands and resonators, but it does not go into a detailed examination of various theories about, or specific uses of, the resonators. Just as you may detract from your singing if you worry too much about locating the exact cause of your self-consciousness, you may not add to the refinement of your vocal tone if you place too much emphasis on a clinical approach to the detailed anatomy of the resonators. But there are some matters that can be helpful if you understand them fully. Keep in mind that a full, resonant tone can occur when "a resonator is in tune with its vibrator. . . ."[3]

[2]William Vennard, *Singing: The Mechanism and the Technic* (New York: Carl Fischer, Inc., 1967), pp. 81–82.

[3]D. Ralph Appleman, *The Science of Vocal Pedagogy* (Bloomington: Indiana University Press, 1967), p. 117.

It can be said that you should ultimately feel resonance in your (1) chest as it is held high, (2) throat as it is in an open position, (3) relaxed pharynx (to give mellowness to your voice), (4) mouth, and (5) sinuses. We have already discussed the proper position of your chest, and you can feel an open throat as you yawn. Your teacher will be your best judge of how much emphasis to place on the use of the pharynx and the sinuses, but the organs involved in the mouth often can be seen in a mirror.

The Tongue.   You can use a mirror to see your tongue and to become acquainted with its action while you are singing. Thus, you can increasingly exercise control over how it works, although there does need to be a period of learning.

If you have a problem with your tongue, it may be because it is too far back in your mouth. Your tongue must assume a variety of positions when you sing, but it will be best for you to consider first its position for the *ah* vowel. Your throat will be most open when your tongue is forward and down, as for an *ah,* and this can be recognized as a usual, desirable position. But there are sounds for which this position is not best, and more specific tongue positions will be given in Units 12–14 for the various vowel and consonant sounds.

The Palates.   Each of us has a hard palate in the upper forward part and a soft palate in the upper back part of the mouth. The hard palate remains fixed, for it is essentially bone. But the soft palate can be shaped, and it is the soft palate that is discussed here.

Your soft palate is the fleshy part of the roof of the mouth near the back, and it can be raised. It is the area where the uvula[4] is located, and when raised or properly stretched, it will offer less resistance to your sung tone. When there is less resistance to the use of the upper resonators, your tone will have more "ring" to it. It is important to use both the upper and the lower resonance areas, but in this instance, your attention is directed to the use of the upper resonance areas.

The Jaw.   When singers speak of the jaw, they are referring to the lower jaw. The lower jaw is movable, and it should remain free and loose. It is connected to many muscles, which can cause the jaw to be held rigidly or support a desirable sense of freedom.

You can use the tips of your fingers to determine if there is rigidness in your lower jaw;[5] a rigid lower jaw will be accompanied by tension in the muscles which control it. If your lower jaw is too tense, you should develop a sense of letting it drop as far as it will move easily, and you should actually move your lower jaw from side to side while you sing. The objective is to free the muscles connected to your lower jaw, which will allow your throat to be more relaxed; the absence of rigidity will allow you to use your resonance areas more successfully.

The Lips.   Your lips should not be pursed or held tightly against your front teeth, or there will be a tendency for your sound to be less alive. Neither should your lips be drawn back as in a smile; such a position will tend to make your tone "white" and, except in some unusual circumstances, is not recommended. The best usual position is for your lips to be relaxed and slightly away from your front teeth.

The Pharynx.   "Immediately above the larynx and extending upward behind the mouth and the nose is a cavity that is called the *pharynx.* . . . Since the pharynx is subject to rather accurate control if the singer is patient enough to learn it, this

----

[4]The uvula is the fleshy lobe in the soft palate.
[5]The fingers should be placed under the jaw.

resonator is most important. Also, it is so near the larynx that it has the first, and therefore the most potent effect upon tone quality."[6]

There is considerable agreement among teachers of singing about the importance of the pharynx, which will become more evident to you later in your study. You will do well to let your teacher advise you how to proceed in detail at this time, but you can begin to achieve the desired result if you will think in terms of singing with unforced openness in your throat.

The Chest.   Your chest should be held high and it should remain quiet. There is some disagreement about calling the chest a resonator, but it is clear that a combination of proper breath support and holding the chest high does create better conditions for improving tone quality. This is the most important point for you to understand at this time.

The Nose and Sinuses.   There seems to be little agreement about the importance of the nose and sinuses as resonators. Some teachers place great importance on their use, and other teachers say they do not enter into this discussion at all. The recommended position for you just now is somewhere between those two extremes, but you should consider the nose and sinuses to be less important than the other areas discussed here.

It *is* generally agreed that nasality is objectionable. You can begin to check yourself for nasality quite easily. Simply hold both nostrils closed while you sing; if you feel restricted, you will clearly be placing too much emphasis on the nose and your sung tone will be too nasal.

Physical Exercises

If you are to sing with a free tone, your body must feel relaxed, a state the following physical exercises will help you achieve.

1. Rotate your shoulders and then let them fall loosely back and down.

2. Gently shake your hands from your wrists.

3. Shake your head easily from side to side; your jaw and lips should be loose and relaxed.

4. Easily move your head up and down to relax the muscles in your neck.

5. Relax the muscles over your cheek bones, and loosen your tongue and lips. Your jaw should feel loose and flexible.

Musical Exercises

You are encouraged to use the preceding exercises each time you practice. Physical relaxation must be present if the following exercises are to be effective.

I

After taking a breath, expel some of it in a "sighlike," light tone. Begin in the upper middle part of your voice and sing with a downward inflection, as in the following musical example. Repeat this exercise several times, and monitor your physical relaxation as well as your breathing and breath support. The dynamic level you use is not really important, but it is important for your sound to be freely and easily produced. Most singers begin by singing *mp* or *mf,* and this exercise essentially is to be spoken. It is not to be sung on any particular pitch.

[6]Vennard, *Singing,* p. 92.

II

Repeat the preceding exercise with the following variation. Allow your lips slowly to open and close several times while you use a *hum* before the vowel. Think of this sound as a *hum* and not as an actual *m* or *n*. Simply feel that you are interrupting the vowel with the *hum,* and repeat the sequence (*hum*-vowel) several times on descending pitches.

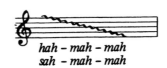

III

Repeat exercise II, but change the vowel now by singing *mah-may-mee-moh-moo* on a descending scale passage. Speak this exercise first, and then sing as in the following musical example.

You should be able to sing with a consistent, free tone on descending scale patterns in the middle part of your voice after you have practiced the first three exercises several times, and it is recommended that you limit your practice to the first three exercises until you have accomplished that goal. After you have sung such musical passages freely and consistently several times, you should include the following exercises in your practice period.

IV

1. Sing *mah-may-mee-moh-moo* on long tones in the middle part of your voice range. Begin with a comfortable pitch, and then lower and raise the pitch by half-steps. Ultimately, you will want to lower and raise the pitch by whole-steps, but you should always keep this exercise in a comfortable pitch range.

2. Sing vowels and *mah-may-mee-moh-moo* while you give your attention to proper breath support and to the singing of consistent, free tones on various pitches.

You should limit your singing to these exercises at first. But it is also recommended that you give your attention to the following art songs as soon as you feel you have been able to sing the exercises with a consistent, free tone.

MUSIC FOR PRACTICE

 May-Day Carol
 If Thou Be Near

9 Registers

The objective of this unit is to present the basic principles in the concept of vocal registers. It may be helpful for you to know that you will focus more on these matters after you have studied longer. However, the discussion here is important to you, the student, because there will often be pitches, as you move up and down in your vocal range, that you will not be able to sing freely. Then you will have found a place in your voice where you should shift from one register to another. You can learn to know when you need to make such an adjustment, but it will take the ear of a trained and knowledgeable teacher to help you make it correctly. The information in this unit is based to a considerable extent on that contained in Vennard and Appleman,[1] and you are referred to those sources for more extensive discussions.

The most easily observed registers are the head and the chest. The head register can be used in the upper part of a singer's range, and the chest register can be used in the lower range. Normally, there will be several notes in the middle range that can be produced by either the head or the chest register. Many Italian masters believed there were only head and chest registers, and Garcia himself (he invented the laryngoscope in 1865) believed in only two registers for some time. But Garcia later broke away from that belief and advocated the three-register (chest, middle, and head) view.[2]

SOME CHARACTERISTICS OF THE CHEST VOICE

The chest register is used in the lower range; it is often called the *heavy voice,* and the vocal bands are thicker than when a singer uses the head voice. "Because of the thickness of the folds the glottis closes firmly and remains closed an appreciable time in each vibration, so that air pressure builds up below and fairly bursts out. Each puff of air opens the glottis almost explosively."[3] The glottis opens at the bottom before it opens at the top, and it closes at the bottom before it closes at the top. Because the vocal bands move relatively large distances, the glottis opens rather wide each time, which is to say the amplitude of vibration is rather great. It takes so long for the opening and closing that the chest voice can be said to be most suitable for the lower tones. Those tones will normally be comparatively loud because pressure builds up in each puff of air; they normally will be rich in harmonic partials because the rippling creates complexity in the puffs of air, and because the greater energy in each cycle makes possible the sounding of other frequencies in addition to the fundamental.[4]

[1]William Vennard, *Singing: The Mechanism and the Technic* (New York: Carl Fischer, Inc., 1967), pp. 52–79; and D . Ralph Appleman, *The Science of Vocal Pedagogy* (Bloomington: Indiana University Press, 1967), pp. 86–99.

[2]Viktor Fuchs, *The Art of Singing and Voice Technique* (New York: London House & Maxwell, 1964), p. 64.

[3]Vennard, *Singing,* p. 66.

[4]Ibid.

When the pitch rises, the muscles continue to be thick while they are working, and this situation requires too much breath power and muscle effort at some point in the singer's scale. At that point, there often will be a momentary loss of control, and the voice will "crack." Such a situation can be avoided if the singer will shift into the use of more head resonance before reaching that point. Such adjustments allow the singer to move up the scale with relative ease.

SOME CHARACTERISTICS OF THE HEAD VOICE

The head voice is lighter than the chest voice. The vocal bands are now relatively thin, and consequently the glottis does not open and close at the bottom first. Often the glottis does not close completely, and when it does, the closure is brief. Higher pitches can be achieved more easily because there is less physical bulk to be moved and the amplitude of the movement is relatively small. The vocal bands offer much less resistance to the breath. Because the edges of the bands are so thin in light mechanism, each puff of air is comparatively simple. The relative weakness of each puff also produces a tone with fewer partials.[5]

COORDINATION OF HEAD AND CHEST REGISTERS

It will be best if you do not expect to use either head or chest tones exclusively. You will have a greater percentage of chest tone when you sing in your lower range, and you will sing with more head tone when you sing in your upper range. But you should not normally think in terms of using only one or the other.

If you try to force the lower resonance and heavy quality into your upper vocal range, you will often have considerable difficulty, possibly even vocal rebellion. Rather, you should shift to more head voice. Then, when you sing in your lower range, you should shift to more chest voice. It will be best if you think in terms of achieving a balance in which the best elements of more than one register are used. That is the ideal toward which you should work, but you should also be aware that it usually takes considerable study before a singer can actually achieve such a balance. It may also be reassuring to know that studies have shown voice teachers to agree about the identification of vocal registers. Teachers do, as a group, recognize those points in a voice where shifts are appropriate.[6]

DIFFERENT APPROACHES TO REGISTERS

The head voice and the chest voice are the two most obvious registers. But there is not universal agreement about how many registers exist. The following discussion summarizes the most often stated concepts.

The One-Register Concept.   This approach holds that there is just one register, which is used over a singer's total vocal range. Those who advocate this concept believe that since the goal is to sing all pitches easily and consistently, the best approach is to look at the total voice as having just one register. They believe that to concentrate on any one particular register will result in different qualities of sound, which do not help develop a total, unified vocal sound.

These teachers may say such things as there are no high or low tones, or all tones should be thought of as being produced on the same level. Their expectation is that students will themselves naturally make needed adjustments if they do not

[5]Ibid., p. 67.
[6]John Large, "Acoustic-Perceptual Evaluation of Register Equalization," *NATS Bulletin* (October 1974), pp. 20–27, 40–41.

fear singing in the various parts of their vocal range, and all pitches will be freely produced.

The Two-Register Concept.   Those who advocate the two-register concept believe that a voice has a light head register and a heavy chest register. They believe that these two registers overlap, and many tones in the middle range can be sung by using either one.

These people also believe that lower voices, basses and contraltos, have such use of chest tone that they use it in all their singing. They say basses and contraltos may use a lighter voice quality in the upper range in order to maintain more flexibility, but some aspect of chest register is used throughout the vocal range.

Moreover, higher voices, sopranos and tenors, always use some aspect of head register; these voices concentrate more on head tones in the upper range, and they bring in some aspect of chest tone in the lower range. But sopranos and tenors use much more head tone than chest tone when they sing.

The Three-Register Concept.   "In the human voice, registration is a physiological and an acoustical fact. Years of research by European teams have contributed evidence of its existence and have verified that all voices have three registers that may be utilized in singing, but this research has contributed little information on their function."[7] These three registers are often called chest, middle, and head, but some teachers use the terms falsetto, head, and chest when they refer to a male singer.

It is generally understood that a bass singer uses the chest register more often, and it is understood that he uses some head register for his high range. The tenor also uses some chest register for his lower pitches and the head register for his upper range. But the tenor uses more head register over a wider compass than does the bass. Also, the tenor often makes more use of the falsetto.

Most teachers agree that the beginning female singer should work to find her middle register. A contralto will more naturally use her chest register, and a soprano will more naturally use her head register. But the teacher should first spend time on finding the middle voice before moving up or down in the range.

VOICE CLASSIFICATION

There should be no hurry to classify your voice when you first begin to study; in fact, there may be some problem in making a hard judgment too soon. There are recognized vocal ranges for each voice classification and there are different voice qualities that can help any singer begin to know where his or her voice should be classified. It is more important for you to determine your voice quality; for example, a tenor should sound like a tenor. However, it has been shown that the middle voice is quite an important area in which to begin training. If the teacher begins to work in the middle voice and then works outward (up and down in pitch), matters such as registers, breaks, range, quality, and so on will tend to develop normally and logically. After those matters have become clearer, the real classification of the voice as a soprano, contralto, tenor, baritone, or bass will also be more obvious.

Professional singers will have a better chance of being successful if they have either some unusually high or some unusually low notes in their vocal range. But as a rule those unusual tones were not always part of the voice. Many years of study are required before one's full vocal potential is realized. Most students do not have unusually high or unusually low voices; most voices cannot sing in extreme ranges. It is the responsibility of the teacher of singing or the choir director to guard against asking singers to sing out of their normal vocal range. It is best to teach students

[7]Appleman, *The Science of Vocal Pedagogy,* p. 86.

in such a way as to bring out the full potential of their voices; also, the teacher should not encourage a student to sing professionally when there is not the talent or the musicianship to draw upon and train.

It is generally true that there are more sopranos than voices in other classifications, and when auditions are held, the problem of supply and demand eliminates more sopranos than contraltos, tenors, baritones, or basses. But a teacher should always resist the temptation to ask a student to sing out of that singer's natural range. Experienced teachers have often seen instances when, for example, a soprano has been pressed into service in the alto section of a choir just because she was a superior musician. Her musicianship gave the alto section more musical stability, which made the soprano an important member of the alto section. But that same soprano may have been singing out of her own voice range. In short, she may have helped the choir, but she may not have helped her own vocal progress. It may help choral singers in schools and universities to think in terms of singing in any range in which their voices can be freely produced. But the moment they begin to force their voices, they are singing out of their natural vocal range and may hinder their own progress.

LIFT OF THE BREATH

Beginning singers can often achieve an improved vocal sound just by working toward more lift of the breath. This concept includes making definite shifts, but it places less emphasis on more radical changes in registration. When a singer moves up in the scale, all shifting will be to a lighter voice production. "As we have seen, the lighter the production the less the intensity for the same amount of breath pressure. Therefore, in order to keep the volume from dropping off, the singer feels the need for an extra surge of breath at the point of shifting."[8] Shifting in this way is quite normal and natural.

But it would be improper to assume that shifts always occur on the same pitches. Range, emotion, and other elements of music also enter into the situation. Because there are many variables, it is quite possible to find several places in a voice where increased lifting of the breath will help. Since several smaller adjustments are normally being made over the vocal range, it is reasonable to expect that there may be several points at which increased lift of the breath will be appropriate.

SUMMARY

There are several different ways to look at the subject of registers—which can cause some confusion in the mind of a beginning student—but there is much support for the three-register concept. The mature singer or teacher may understand that the differences in these various ways of looking at registers are not really so great. The most basic points for beginning students to remember are that shifts are to be made as they sing up and down in their vocal range, and that there are not sufficient data to document exactly how often the adjustments should be made.

If you remember that each singer is unique, you will not worry so much about standardizing procedures. You will focus on working freely and naturally. But it will be an advantage to work with an experienced teacher whose ear can be depended on to detect those points at which vocal adjustments need to be made.

Musical Exercises _____

You should practice those exercises that are appropriate to your voice, and you should practice them often enough to recognize where you must shift in order to

[8]Vennard, *Singing*, p. 77.

continue singing freely and with a full sound. Of course, you should move the key, if necessary, to take advantage of your own best range.

uh oh uh   uh oh uh
uh ah uh   uh ah uh
ee oh ee   ee oh ee
ee ah ee   ee ah ee

etc.

(Sing this exercise on each vowel.)   *etc.*

(Sing this exercise on each vowel.)   *etc.*

(Sing this exercise on each vowel.)

(Sing this exercise on each vowel.)   *etc.*

(Sing this exercise on each vowel.)   *etc.*

10 *Legato*

and Sustained Tones

Your objective in this unit is to learn to sing with controlled legato tone, as is required in most vocal music.

You have already learned about good posture, controlling your breath, and singing with a free tone, and you should always be attentive to those matters. Singing with sustained tones does not require you to learn a completely new set of principles, but your legato singing will be better if you will bring together those related principles already learned. Specifically, it is recommended that you first sing legato vowel sounds in a comfortable voice range and then coordinate your increased ability to sing beginning consonant and vowel sounds. Of course, your legato singing will improve as you improve your breath control.

Much good music utilizes texts in English, but Italian diction is considered by many singers to be more compatible with pure vowel sounds. For that reason, English and Italian are often the first two languages sung by students. But you may want to substitute music with a text in French or German if one of these is your first language.

As has already been said, singing sustained tones is not a subject to be isolated; it includes breath support, diction, and resonance, and those topics are discussed elsewhere. You should not be surprised by this interdependence, for all topics studied should ultimately contribute to how well you sing.

The singing of legato and sustained tones is discussed separately because it is such singing that you will be called on to perform most often. It has been said that legato is as important to a singer as the barre is to a dancer. Legato singing should be smooth, with a slow and sustained movement and a continuous tone. Any imperfection in your basic tone production will tend to be magnified when you sing legato; therefore, you should practice legato from the very beginning of your study.

AN EVEN SCALE

The development of an even scale is of central importance to beautiful legato singing, and you can achieve an even scale only through diligent practice. Essentially, you will acquire consistent tone production when you learn to eliminate accumulations of tension, for tension may be a contributing factor in vocal breaks, sudden changes of quality, or soft spots in your voice.

Your sung scale will often be more even if you do not think of your voice as going up or down for extremely high or low pitches. To squeeze high notes or to reach down for low notes is one of the most usual causes of tension and unevenness in a voice. Actually, you should give your high tones more depth by using more low resonance areas, and you should give your low tones more "ring" by using more upper resonance areas. Even when you sing an octave, for example, there should be no sudden change of quality; nothing radical should happen in your throat even when you sing wide intervals. It may be helpful for you to feel that your low tones are produced on the same physical level as your high tones. Again, there should be no physical feeling of "reaching" for high or low notes.

THE VOCAL LINE

When you sing consecutive legato tones, you are said to be singing a vocal line. It is fundamentally important for you to be able to maintain a sustained vocal line. As soon as you are able to sing sustained tones, you should include in your practice musical exercises that require you to link two or more notes without interruption.

You will get your best results when you (1) limit your legato singing to vowels that move by step or intervals up to a perfect fifth; (2) add more extended exercises on the five basic vowels (see Unit 12); (3) add beginning consonant and vowel combinations after achieving step 2; and (4) add simple songs after you have practiced all the preceding steps.

You will progress more quickly if you include those four steps in your practice period. Of course, you will ultimately require less time to move through the first steps, and you will then be able to spend more time singing actual songs. At that point, the first steps will be accomplished in the few minutes you spend warming up your voice for each day's singing. However, you should not expect to omit entirely any of the steps.

You should expect to have more difficulty singing a legato line when consonants are involved instead of just vowel sounds. However, texts do contain consonants, and it is ultimately necessary for every singer to learn how to handle consonant sounds successfully.

Portamento.   The use of the portamento is not of primary importance to you in your first year of study, but a brief discussion of the term is included here so that you will know the similarities and differences between it and legato. "Portamento is closely related to legato. The word comes from the Italian *portare,* to carry. Legato means the smooth linking of two or more notes, whereas portamento means a slower sliding from one note to the next."[1] When portamento is required, the voice glides through all pitches present between the two written pitches of an interval. Its proper use is to move so rapidly through the intermediate pitches that those persons listening will not notice them. Portamento can help musical expression in some music, but its use can also lead to problems when it is not properly executed. For that reason, it is recommended that you now concentrate on perfecting your legato singing; you should leave emphasis on the use of portamento until later in your singing career.

Musical Exercises

The four steps to be followed in learning how to sing with a legato tone were listed earlier in this unit, and the following musical exercises use the order recommended there. You should practice these exercises until you can sing them quite easily.

I

Sing the five basic vowels, as listed in Unit 12, in short exercises until you can move by steps and intervals as far as a perfect fifth without any apparent change in or deterioration of your sung tone. (The following exercises may also be sung in octaves.)

[1]Viktor Fuchs, *The Art of Singing and Voice Technique* (New York: London House & Maxwell, 1964), p. 104.

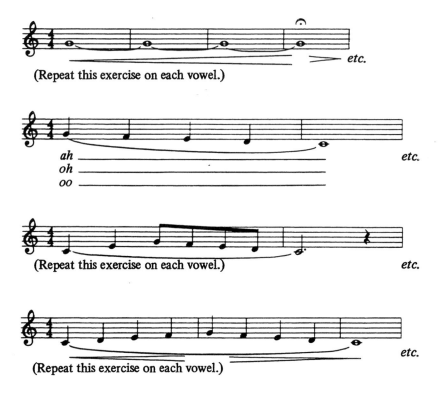

(Repeat this exercise on each vowel.)

ah _____
oh _____
oo _____   etc.

(Repeat this exercise on each vowel.)   etc.

(Repeat this exercise on each vowel.)

II

Add the singing of longer exercises on the five basic vowels.

(Repeat this exercise on each vowel.)   etc.

(Repeat this exercise on each vowel.)   etc.

(Repeat this exercise on each vowel.)

III

Add beginning consonants to the vowel sounds used in the preceding two steps.

mah   meh   mee   moh   moo

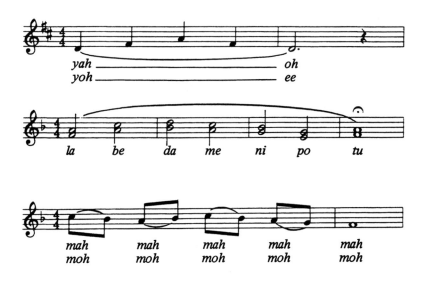

yah ——————————— oh
yoh ——————————— ee

la   be   da   me   ni   po   tu

mah   mah   mah   mah   mah
moh   moh   moh   moh   moh

IV

Sing those songs recommended at the end of this unit.

In summary, the musical exercises included here are representative; you should always think in terms of possibly transposing them to be more compatible with your own particular vocal requirements.

Legato exercises should be a part of your practice from the very beginning of your study; although you will become more proficient as you continue your study, you should not expect to master legato singing to such a degree that you may discontinue these exercises. When you have mastered the four steps outlined in this unit, you will have moved on to a more advanced level of music making.

MUSIC FOR PRACTICE

What If a Day
Nina

11 Prevention of Voice Disorders

Robert W. Bastian, M.D.[1]

It is more effective to build a fence at the top of a cliff than to park an ambulance at the bottom. (Source Unknown)

INTRODUCTION

Singers properly concentrate on developing technical and artistic skills. But most of them will be afflicted at one time or another with a physical problem that can thwart those skills. To help vocalists avoid such problems, this unit reviews some basic principles of voice care, with a special emphasis on prevention. Readers with no background in the anatomy of the vocal folds may wish, before proceeding, to review Box 11-1, entitled "The Vocal Fold Mucosa: What Is It?" on pages 49–52.

Fortunately, however inconvenient their timing, common *acute* vocal maladies, such as those associated with viral upper respiratory tract infections and allergies, respond well to a physician's treatments or even to the simple passage of time. But the author's studies and observations reveal that a significant percentage of *chronic* vocal problems in singers involve an unintended but self-inflicted, and then surprisingly unrecognized, injury to the vocal fold mucosa, resulting, over time, in chronic swelling. It is these kinds of chronic swellings that are not only avoidable but also usually more stubborn to resolve than some of the acute medical conditions that plague singers.

The focus of this unit is on means of prevention and, failing prevention, early detection of vocal fold mucosal swellings before they become established nodules or polyps. Also looked at are brief general guidelines concerning selected medical disorders, such as upper respiratory infections and allergies (see Box 11-2, "Common Medical Conditions"). Self-diagnosis and treatment may be appropriate at the onset of vocal problems, but singers are advised to seek the advice of their own physicians for individualized medical care.

Since it is more effective to build a fence at the top of a cliff than to park an ambulance at the bottom (see Figure 11-1), singers would do well to construct for themselves three "fences" at the top of the cliff of voice problems: (1) practice of good vocal hygiene, (2) utilization of appropriate voice production, and (3) knowledge of the symptoms of vocal fold mucosal swelling. Each of these fences alone provides strong protection against development of chronic mucosal swelling. But

[1]Dr. Bastian is a professor in the Department of Otolaryngology—Head and Neck Surgery—at Loyola University of Chicago (Medical Campus) in Maywood, Illinois.

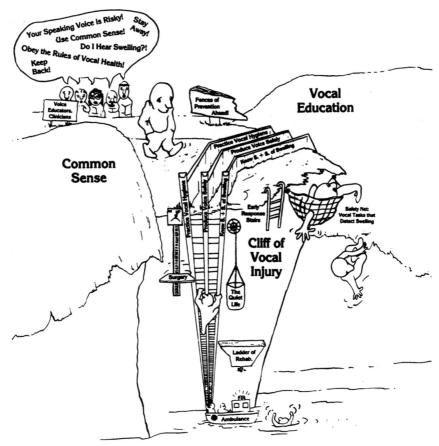

Figure 11-1 "It is more effective to build a fence at the top of a cliff than to station an ambulance at the bottom." *Used by permission of Robert W. Bastian, M.D.*

Box 11-1 The Vocal Fold Mucosa: What Is It?

As skin covers the outside of the body, *mucosa* serves to cover internal structures that make up the mouth, throat, larynx, and so forth. Consequently, the covering or surface layer of the vocal folds is the *vocal fold mucosa*. It is similar to the smooth, wet tissue one feels when running the tip of the tongue over the inner surface of the cheek.

To simplify, the mucosa is the main "moving part" during vocal fold vibration, analogous to the mucosa of trumpet players' lips while playing. The mucosa of each vocal fold is designed to withstand even millions of "collisions" with the other vocal fold each day. In fact, the vocal fold mucosa of a person singing A below middle C will vibrate or collide 220 times per second, 13,200 times per minute, and 792,000 times per hour of continuous sound!

If vibratory collisions are too forceful, if the mucosa is made vulnerable by infection, allergy, or dryness, if the total number of collisions is simply too great, or if a combination of those stresses "overwhelms" the mucosa's tolerance, it will swell as a reaction to vibratory trauma. Acute swelling, mainly representing fluid accumulation, will disappear with voice rest for as little as a day or two. However, if the conditions that led to acute swelling continue, the swelling becomes more stubborn and can require months of conservative treatment or, in unusual circumstances, surgery to resolve. (See Figures 11-2 and 11-3.)

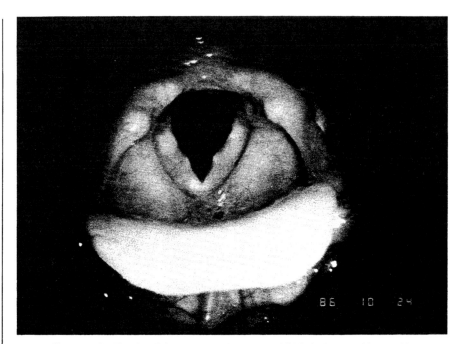

Figure 11-2. Vocal nodules, as seen with the vocal folds in the breathing position. *Used by permission of Robert W. Bastian, M.D.*

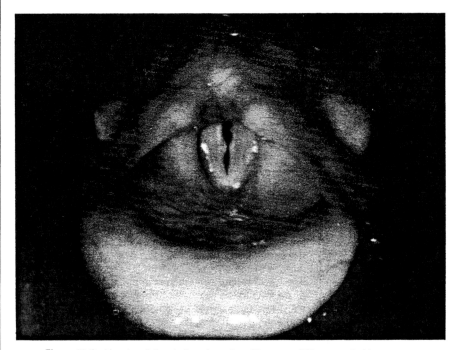

Figure 11-3 Vocal nodules during phonation. These would be expected to cause increased singing effort, loss of some of the upper voice, and onset delays with soft singing. With more vigorous singing, the vocal folds are squeezed closer together and the sound tends to clear. This person may not have a hoarse singing voice. *Used by permission of Robert W. Bastian, M.D.*

Box 11-2   Common Medical Conditions

The following is intended only to orient singers to the nature and usual treatments of some common medical conditions. Singers experiencing the following problems should seek the best medical attention available.

Upper Respiratory Infections

Cause: Most commonly, one of numerous viruses; they may progress to a bacterial infection of nose and sinuses (sinusitis), larynx (laryngitis), throat (tonsillitis or pharyngitis), or lungs (bronchitis or pneumonia).

Symptoms: Profuse nasal discharge, sneezing, nasal congestion, postnasal drip. There may be a progression to mild sore throat, hoarseness, and cough. Mild fever may or may not be present, along with generalized aches and pains. The bacterial infections referred to above may cause a greater degree of malaise, pain, fever, and infected-looking mucus.

Common treatments: Rest, healthful diet, and liberal fluid intake; steam inhalations; passage of time. Nasal symptoms may be treated when necessary with mild vasoconstrictors applied to the nose for no more than three days. Nasal decongestants taken in pill form tend to dry the larynx, too, and should be avoided, particularly when significant voice use is necessary. Voice use should be reduced to a prudent level, because the vocal fold mucosa is usually more vulnerable to swelling caused by vibratory "collisions" even when frank laryngitis does not seem to be present. When there are signs of bacterial infection (significant fever, pain, or discolored mucus), antibiotic treatment may be in order.

Allergy and Asthma

Cause: One or more environmental substances, such as dust, tree, grass, or weed pollens, mold spores, animal danders, and so forth. They may also be caused by certain foods, such as milk, eggs, chocolate, nuts, and berries. Asthma may sometimes be unrelated to allergies.

Symptoms: They may be highly variable. Most common symptoms include sneezing, watery nasal discharge, itchy eyes, nose, or palate, and postnasal drainage. Specific laryngeal symptoms are relatively less common than nasal symptoms. Asthma symptoms may vary from almost-unrecognized breathing symptoms, cough, and sputum production, to severe and obvious wheezing and shortness of breath.

Treatments: For the mild, occasional allergy sufferer, symptomatic treatment may be justified, with carefully selected nondrying antihistamines and topical steroid nasal sprays taken as directed by a physician who understands the details of their use by singers. More frequent or troublesome allergy symptoms, and any suggestion of asthma, indicate the need for thorough workup and management under the care of one or more of the following: an allergist, a pulmonary specialist, or an otolaryngologist (ear, nose, and throat physician) specializing in allergy.

Acid Reflux Laryngitis/Pharyngitis

Cause: The reflux (backward flow) of acid from the stomach up the esophagus and into the back of the throat and larynx, usually during sleep.

Symptoms: A chronic dry, scratchy, raw, or irritated throat. Often these symptoms are worse in the morning and are relieved somewhat as the day progresses. One may also experience a great deal of morning phlegm, a chronic irritative cough, an unusually low-pitched morning voice, and the need for prolonged warmup (the last symptom can also be a symptom of mucosal swelling). Persons with acid reflux may sometimes, but certainly not always, experience intermittent heartburn to suggest their tendency to acid reflux.

Treatments: Eat the last food of the day no fewer than three hours before retiring, so that the stomach is relatively empty at bedtime. Avoid caffeine, alcohol, and spicy foods, all of which may exaggerate one's tendency to acid reflux. Utilize four- to six-inch bedblocks between the floor and the headposts of the bed, so as to place the entire bed on a slight downward slant from head to foot. (Gravity thereby helps to keep stomach contents where they belong.) Take a bedtime dose of Gaviscon, an over-the-counter antacid. (A physician may prescribe a more powerful antisecretory medication for bedtime use when the indications of acid reflux are strong.)

Transient Vocal Fold Mucosal Swelling from Acute Abuse/Overuse
Obstinate Vocal Fold Mucosal Swelling from Long-term Abuse/Overuse

See Fence 3: "Know the Symptoms of Vocal Fold Swelling," and "The Safety Net: A Vocal Task That Detects Swelling." See also Box 11–1.

what about singers who have already failed or may in the future fail to erect or observe the fences? For them, this unit provides a "safety net," a task that helps detect vocal fold swelling early, when treatment will have a high rate of success. The singer who takes the trouble to master all three fences and the safety net is unlikely ever to be taken unawares by a diagnosis of nodules or other forms of vocal fold mucosal swelling.

A word to overly scrupulous readers: The human voice is in many ways quite rugged, and singing may at times require aggressive voice production. It is therefore not intended that student singers become obsessed with the effect of daily activity on their voices. At the same time, the suggestions that follow may serve to remind you that the serious singer is called to a life of discipline in order to maintain the voice in the best condition possible.

FENCE 1: PRACTICE GOOD VOCAL HYGIENE

This simply means establishing consistent conditions or practices in your life that maintain vocal health. For example:

Avoid or keep risky voice use to a minimum. Prolonged cheering at a noisy outdoor athletic event is an obvious example. Another is participating in extended conversations in noisy surroundings, such as at a boisterous party replete with loud music. Yet another is teaching a vocal part to the altos while also directing the entire choir. Because of the masking effect of background noise in all these situations, singers may not realize the extent to which they are abusing or overusing the voice.

Do not consume or use substances that are known to cause vocal deterioration. Of course, tobacco and marijuana are prime examples; they are known to dry and irritate the vocal fold mucosa, and even to promote polyp formation (not to mention the more grave long-term risks). Another culprit is alcohol. Together with overdoing it vocally, alcohol—particularly for some singers—seems to potentiate a well-known, stubborn condition—chronic laryngitis. Caffeine in coffee, tea, and many soft drinks, by its weak diuretic effect, may cause mild dehydration; relative dryness of the vocal fold mucosa that follows may leave it more vulnerable to the rigors of vibration. Caffeine may also exacerbate acid reflux laryngitis in singers prone to this condition (see Box 11–2).

Various legitimate medications (certain antihistamines are prominent examples) may also have drying effects on the vocal fold mucosa. Some doctors believe that because aspirin and other related anti-inflammatory medications have some "blood-thinning" activity, use of those medications may cause vocal fold hemorrhages, though uncommon even among aspirin users, to be more serious.

Finally, various illicit drugs, by their tendency to reduce general effectiveness, may be incompatible with a singer's fullest development.

Consume adequate amounts of fluids. Approximately eight cups of fluid per day is enough for most people under usual circumstances. The adequacy of this amount is assured if the urine is relatively pale in color. Some singers overlook the importance of a steady supply of fluid, as opposed to consuming large amounts of fluid at intervals, with many "dry" hours in between.

Be aware of the manifestations of acid reflux laryngitis, caused by migration of stomach acid upward into the throat and posterior larynx during sleep, and institute antireflux measures for any suspicion of their occurrence. (See Box 11–2.)

Optimize the management of medical conditions such as allergies, asthma, and infections. Beyond following a physician's advice carefully, the singer should monitor especially closely the amount and the circumstances of voice use during "flare-ups" of any of these conditions, even when the voice does not seem to be directly involved by laryngitis, for the vocal fold mucosa is more vulnerable to swelling during these times.

FENCE 2: UTILIZE APPROPRIATE VOICE PRODUCTION

The purposes of voice training are not only to expand vocal capabilities and to learn to make aesthetically pleasing vocal sounds, but also to establish a high degree of coordination and efficiency between the *power supply* (muscles of inspiration and expiration acting on the lungs), the *sound source* (larynx), and the *resonators* (mostly the spaces and structures of the upper respiratory tract, such as throat, nose, tongue, and palate). If one succeeds in meeting these goals through voice training, one should learn to make each sung sound not only beautifully but also with the least possible risk of injury to the mucosa.

Unfortunately, the importance of efficient and "safe" voice production for *speaking* is often overlooked by singers. Many young people sing extremely well but are careless with how they speak. The singer has but one voice for both singing and speaking.

The author has evaluated hundreds of female singers whose habitual pitch for speaking is between D and G below middle C, often within a few semitones of the lowest pitch they can possibly produce. Arguably more important than pitch itself is the fact that these women may also speak in what could be described as a strong chest register, which of course requires an extremely different kind of voice production from that used for classical singing. The author has observed among such women both a relatively high incidence of mucosal swelling and a tendency for their speaking-voice production to "interfere" with that used for singing. One dramatic example of the negative impact inappropriate speaking-voice production had on the voice was that of a coloratura soprano whose average pitch for speaking was d

(below middle C: 𝄢) and whose speech and laughter were positively baritonal.

It is no wonder that she was developing chronic vocal fold swellings and losing some of the upper part of the voice!

Many speech pathologists and interested voice teachers offer training of voice production for speech.

FENCE 3: KNOW THE SYMPTOMS OF VOCAL FOLD SWELLING

Occasionally, young singers come to believe that their vocal frustrations must be the result of some physical disorder. When thorough functional and medical evaluations by voice teacher, laryngologist, and speech pathologist rule out a physical cause, such singers need to be convinced that these difficulties are actually technical and will respond to further vocal study.

However, the author more frequently has encountered frustrated singers who believe that their persistent vocal limitations are "technical," when in actuality there is a physical cause. The following are some of the explanations of symptoms the author has received from singers before they were diagnosed as having chronic swelling of the vocal fold mucosa. "I have just been tired recently." "My voice is growing." "I am really a mezzo." "It's a really big voice, and that's why I can only sing loudly up high." "I am learning to support my voice better to get rid of the breathiness in my upper voice."

In fact, many singers mistakenly believe that if they are not hoarse, they do not have swelling of their vocal fold mucosa. The following list of symptoms is offered to expand the singer's understanding of symptoms that may be caused by vocal fold mucosal swelling. Because some of these symptoms may also be technically based, see the next section—"The Safety Net"—for additional help in differentiating between physical and technical causes. Of course, the singer with one or more of the following symptoms on a significant and persistent basis should seek the advice of a voice teacher and other voice specialists.

1. *Increased effort required for singing, as compared with that required earlier.* One patient with this and other symptoms found to be caused by vocal nodules said, "I can still sing well at times, but singing is too much work to be fun anymore."

2. *Deterioration of high soft singing and staccato.* Not infrequently, a singer with swelling will deny any loss of high notes ("I can still sing high C"), only to admit, when questioned closely, that the upper notes can only be sung loudly and with a great deal of "support." (See "The Safety Net.")

3. *Loss of endurance.* Students who are singing very little may lose endurance as a result of being out of shape vocally, particularly if they are also inactive as speakers. However, singers who are very busy vocally and who note that the voice becomes "tired" or husky more easily than before should entertain the possibility of swelling.

4. *Breathiness and corresponding tendency to run out of air.* Technical faults are a prominent cause of breathiness. However, when escapage of air perceived as breathiness becomes *worse* rather than better the higher one sings, the cause may be swelling.

5. *Day-to-day variability of vocal quality and capabilities.* All singers, and particularly those who are just starting their vocal studies, experience this phenomenon. In fact, one of the marks of the highly trained singer is the ability to sing well in spite of such day-to-day variations. However, well-trained singers who note, on a consistent basis, greater than usual fluctuations of vocal capabilities and quality should consider mucosal swelling as a possible cause.

6. *Hoarseness, harshness.* In the author's experience, when these symptoms become obvious on a chronic basis, and particularly when the speaking voice is also affected, swelling has developed beyond the subtle or mild stage. When that happens, the singer has already overlooked or misinterpreted some of the earlier symptoms of swelling listed here.

THE SAFETY NET: A VOCAL TASK THAT DETECTS SWELLING

For any singer who ignores the importance of the fences of good vocal hygiene, appropriate voice production, and alertness to symptoms of swelling, a "safety net" is provided in the form of a vocal task that detects mucosal swelling reliably. This task is also helpful in differentiating between physical and technical causes of various vocal symptoms listed earlier. It is one of three devised and tested by the author along with speech and language pathology colleagues Anat Keidar, Ph.D., and Katherine Verdolini, M.A. This particular task was designed so that both trained and untrained singers with *normal vocal folds* can sing it successfully. In both singers and nonsingers, the ability to perform the task correlates well with presence, absence, or degree of swelling. Poor performance, therefore, tends to suggest a physical rather than a technical cause, whether one is an advanced student or a beginner. However, it should be stressed that this task is described to help the singer know when to consult teacher, speech pathologist, and laryngologist for formal evaluation regarding the possibility of vocal fold swelling, and is not sufficient by itself to come to an absolute conclusion about whether the problem is physical or technical.

THE TASK: THE FIRST PHRASE OF "HAPPY BIRTHDAY"

Performance Instructions

1. *Sing it at a "boy soprano pianissimo."* In other words, sing more softly than you ever would sing for the purposes of voice training or public performance. Because a singer can conceal the manifestations of swelling by simply singing more loudly, or with "more support," this task must be performed extremely softly!

2. *Concentrate on the upper part of the voice.* For women, that means especially between c″ (𝄞) and c‴ (𝄞). For men, it means mainly the lower part of the falsetto register—or, for those few men in whom falsetto voice has never been present, the highest, lightest voice possible.

Indicators of Possible Vocal Fold Swelling

1. *Inability to sing the task at all unless one is singing relatively loudly, even if the voice sounds clear at this loud dynamic.*

2. *Slight breathiness that becomes more pronounced as one approaches the top of the falsetto or head register (high C for most women).* To be significant, this breathiness need not be more than a faint sound of escaping air present all of the time, or just at the start of each new syllable. If the voice gets *less* breathy as one goes higher in the voice, swelling is not likely. Breathiness in the male falsetto is not quite as sensitive an indicator unless it is a new finding.

3. *Delayed vocal onsets.* The singer with this manifestation of swelling will note, when singing as instructed above, that a fraction of a second (or longer) passes between the intended onset of the sound and when it actually does begin. During this momentary (or longer) onset delay, one can often hear the faint passage of air without any actual vocal sound. When this manifestation becomes severe, entire syllables may be lost from the "Happy Birthday" task. Remember that onset delays will tend to disappear when one sings more loudly; consequently, one must insist on singing extremely softly! Some men who do not have swelling may note a tendency toward delayed vocal onsets at very high falsetto pitches. Therefore, the lower falsetto takes on more importance for those men.

SUGGESTIONS FOR RESPONDING TO SYMPTOMS AND MANIFESTATIONS THAT RAISE THE QUESTION OF SWELLING

Singers who detect some of the symptoms and manifestations of swelling might fall into one of several groups. The first group may experience *acute, subtle to mild* symptoms or manifestations of swelling. A person in this group will want to reduce voice use to prudent levels until symptoms and manifestations go away (usually within a couple of days). Frequent episodes of acute symptoms suggest the need for modification of lifestyle and voice production or treatment of contributing medical conditions.

A second group of singers may note *acute, moderate to severe* symptoms and manifestations of swelling. The singer in this category should rest the voice immediately and as much as possible. Failure to return to normal within a few days calls for early consultation with one's voice teacher and possibly with a laryngologist.

Upon reading the preceding sections, a few singers may begin to suspect that mild or even severe symptoms with which they have been struggling technically for several months, or even years, may in fact have a physical cause. After appropriate consultation with their voice teachers, these singers should seek to resolve this question by undergoing the most sophisticated medical evaluation available in their areas.

It bears emphasizing that a chronic swelling such as vocal nodules is not a tumor or disease but is, rather, a reactive swelling somewhat analogous to a callus on the palm of a hand. Accordingly, one looks first to the *general and vocal behavior of the singers* for the causes of their chronic mucosal swelling. Treatment of each of these conditions ordinarily begins with attention to Fences 1 and 2 as rehabilitative rather than only preventative measures (see those sections). The author also suggests a few weeks of moderately reduced voice use, particularly for speaking. Attention to medical conditions, such as allergy, round out the treatment plan. The response to conservative treatment (appropriate medical treatments, good vocal hygiene, optimization of voice production for both speaking and singing, and reduction of voice use) depends on the duration, severity, and type of the swelling, along with the afflicted singer's compliance with treatments.

Singers sometimes regard the diagnosis of a chronic form of vocal fold swelling as the end of their aspirations as singers. On the contrary, the overwhelming majority of singers can be rehabilitated if they are willing to avail themselves of expert guidance. However, if the swellings persist, accompanied by unacceptable symptoms and limitations in spite of a high degree of compliance with a prolonged trial of conservative approaches, precise removal of swellings can in most cases restore the voice to normal or near-normal condition. The author believes the risk of such surgery, when the surgeon is experienced in performing microsurgery on the vocal folds of singers, is acceptably low for singers who cannot rehabilitate to their satisfaction after a lengthy trial of the best conservative treatments available. Obviously, the singer is advised to seek the opinions of several professionals and perhaps of other singers who have undergone this kind of surgery before making such an important decision.

SUMMARY

The author believes that singers need not face a diagnosis of chronic vocal fold mucosal swelling if they establish the practices of good vocal hygiene, appropriate voice production for both speech and singing, and knowledge of the symptoms of mucosal swelling. And there is hope for rehabilitation if they do fall into vocal distress.

12 *Basic Vowel Sounds*

The objective of this unit is to convey specific information about those vowels most often used in singing.

Texts are made up of consonants and vowels, but the vowels consume more singing time than do the consonants. Listed below are the five basic vowel sounds to be discussed in this unit.

Sound:	ah	eh	ee	oh	oo
Webster:[1]	ä	e	ē	ō	ü
IPA:[2]	[ɑ]	[ɛ]	[i]	[o]	[u]

THE BASIS OF PRONUNCIATION

You have sung the *ah, eh, ee, oh,* and *oo* sounds in the exercises at the close of preceding units. Vowel sounds serve as the very basis of a singer's pronunciation, and you will be well advised to practice them sufficiently to become intimately acquainted with them. Since the singing of consonants is accomplished quickly, they take relatively little sung time. Most of a singer's time is consumed in singing vowels, and any incorrect, or unnatural, vowel color will be easily heard. Obviously, such faulty vowel sounds can detract from your effectiveness as a singer.

Most people do not give enough attention to how vowel sounds are produced. Since singers "feel" how their various vocal tones differ, you should first become acquainted with how each vowel is formed. It will become increasingly important for you to learn to sing the different vowels consistently in all parts of your vocal range. This progress may take months or years to accomplish, but the objective now is to obtain the information you need for a sure, solid foundation on which to build.

Written:	a
Sound:	*ah*
	ä
IPA:	[ɑ]

The sound to use in your sung exercises is *ah,* as in *father.* Remember that the *a* will sometimes be found in such words as *man* [æ] and *day* [ɛɪ]; also, an *ah* sound can be heard in such words as *God* and *hot.* But it is the *ah* sound as found in *father* and *heart* that is most basic to your study of singing; it is sometimes called the Italian *ah.*

The *ah* sound is the most open of the five vowel sounds. You will achieve the

---

[1]*Webster's Third New International Dictionary of the English Language, Unabridged* (Springfield, Mass.: G. & C. Merriam Co., 1971). The Webster symbol is listed above the IPA symbol in all charts.

[2]International Phonetic Alphabet; it may be found in *The Principles of the International Phonetic Association* (International Phonetic Association, University College, London: 1949).

approximate positions of the tongue, jaw, and lips when you yawn (be aware that yawning may produce tension), but the following points will give you more specific information:

1. Your lips will be rounded and quite relaxed. You should simply permit your lips to open comfortably; there should be no feeling of tenseness. Ideally, this position will be so natural that you will not need to focus on the position of your lips.
2. Your lower jaw will be dropped but quite relaxed. You will feel tension if your lower jaw is dropped too far. As for the lips, you will ultimately hope to find such a natural position for the lower jaw that you will no longer need to engage in any kind of manipulation.
3. The tip of your tongue will be forward and will gently touch the back of your lower gum. Your tongue should be down far enough to be slightly grooved, and it should be forward enough to allow your throat to open. (The back of the tongue forms a part of the forward wall of the throat.)
4. You should take care not to protrude the lips.

WORDS TO SPEAK ALOUD

charm harm dart heart jar far calm dark psalm

EXAMPLES FROM MUSIC TEXTS

the everlasting F*a*ther
He w*a*tching over Israel

Written: e
Sound: *eh*   *ee*
                   ē
IPA: [ɛ]   [i]

This vowel has two different sounds, as found in (1) *me* and *reveal* and (2) *led* and *head.* In singing the *ee* sound, as in *me,* your mouth will necessarily be in a relatively closed position, and the following points will serve to guide the position of your tongue, lips, and jaw:

1. The tip of your tongue will be slightly raised and will touch the back of your lower front teeth; the back portion of your tongue will be raised.
2. Your lips will be parted slightly, and the lower lip will feel a slight downward pull from the very center.
3. Your lower jaw will always be relaxed.

When you sing the *eh* sound, as in *led,* you should observe the following points:

1. The tip of your tongue will be down. If it is raised at all, it will be raised less than for the *ee* sound in *me.*
2. Your lips will be parted more than for the *ee* sound. They will be slightly forward, but less far than for the *ee* sound, and your lower lip will have more of a downward pull from the center than it has when you sing an *ee* sound.
3. Your lower jaw will always be relaxed, and it will be dropped farther than for the *ee* sound.

WORDS TO SPEAK ALOUD

we three each please weep see be he leave keep beat
west went quest lend end fed led bed said tread

EXAMPLES FROM MUSIC TEXTS

and H*e* shall purify
All w*e* like sh*ee*p

Behold and *see*
D*ea*th is now a w*e*lcome gu*e*st

Written: i
Sound: *ih*
i

IPA: [ɪ]

The sound you will use most in your exercises is the *i*[3] as in *it*, but this sound is also found as a part of the diphthong in *day.* (Diphthongs will be discussed in Unit 14.)

Many singers do not differentiate between the vowel sounds in *it* and *wed;* other words, such as *pin* and *pen*, may fall victim to the same problem. In most instances, you will pronounce your words well if you know the specific sound to be sung and then are careful to sing with the proper tongue, lip, and jaw positions. Observe the following points in singing this vowel sound:

1.   The tip of your tongue will be against your lower front teeth; it will not be raised as much as for the *ee* sound.
2.   Your upper lip will be pointed slightly forward so that it will not lie against your upper front teeth.
3.   Your lower jaw will be dropped farther than for the *ee* sound, but it will not be dropped as far as for the *eh* sound. It will be helpful for you to say *ee, ih, eh* aloud and notice the different positions of your lower jaw.

WORDS TO SPEAK ALOUD

*h*i*m s*i*t m*i*d l*i*ft s*i*nce w*i*nter m*i*ss p*i*ty sl*i*pped*

EXAMPLES FROM MUSIC TEXTS

ev'ry mountain and h*i*ll made low
let the sp*i*r*i*t of th*i*s child return
L*i*ft up your heads, O ye gates
S*i*nce by man came death

Written: o
Sound: *oh*
o̅

IPA: [o]

The jaw position for this vowel sound is very close to that used for the *ah* sound. If you have difficulty with it, it is recommended that you begin by singing an *ah* sound on a medium pitch and then round your lips to form an *oh* sound without interrupting your tone. Although this may not be the exact jaw position you will use later, it can be a helpful exercise when you are first becoming ac-quainted with your feeling for the *oh* sound. This sound may also be found as a part of a diphthong, which is discussed in Unit 14. Observe the following points when you sing this vowel sound:

1.   The back of your tongue will be more raised than for the *ah* sound.
2.   The tip of your tongue will be forward, touching your lower gum.
3.   Your lips will be more rounded than for the *ah* sound, and the rounding will be com-paratively large. They will be slightly pointed, and they will essentially form an oval shape.
4.   Your jaw will be relaxed and down.

---

[3]It should also be noted that the written *i* in Italian sounds very close to the written *e* as found in *me* and *reveal.*

WORDS TO SPEAK ALOUD

oh over obey boat hold protect moan

EXAMPLES FROM MUSIC TEXTS

Behold the Lamb of God
they have spoken falsely
Take His yoke upon you
Lift up your heads, *O* ye gates

Written: u
Sound: *oo*
                ü
IPA: [u]

This vowel may be less open than either the *ah* or the *oh* sound, but the position of your lower jaw will be about the same for each. In fact, the position of your lower jaw does not change greatly for any of these five vowels; the greater change is in the position of your tongue, lips, or both. Observe the following points when you sing this vowel sound:

1. The back of your tongue will be arched, but it will not be arched as much as for the *ee* sound.
2. The tip of your tongue will touch your lower gum.
3. Your lips will be pointed forward into a pout; they will be rounded, with a small opening. The sides of your lips will be kept narrow so that they form a circle, but not a slit, and both lips will be allowed to move away from your teeth.

WORDS TO SPEAK ALOUD

too soon choose who flute prove true do

EXAMPLES FROM MUSIC TEXTS

But wh*o* may abide
Wh*o* is the King of glory

Musical Exercises

Remember that you should move the pitch of the exercises up or down if another key is more comfortable for your voice. (The following exercises may also be sung in octaves.)

ah	eh	ee	oh	oo	etc.
eh	ee	oh	oo	ah
ee	oh	oo	ah	eh

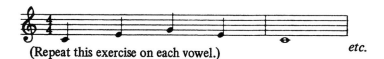

(Repeat this exercise on each vowel.)   *etc.*

(Repeat this exercise on each vowel.)   *etc.*

(Repeat this exercise on each vowel.)   *etc.*

ah   eh   ee   oh   oo   etc.

ah   eh   ee   oh   oo   etc.

ah   eh   ee   oh   oo   etc.

13 *Consonants*

The objective of this unit is to give you specific information about the consonants you will find in a text.

Correctly formed vowels help any singer produce a free tone, but consonants are also important. Consonants are sung much more quickly and must be clearly articulated if a soloist or a chorus is to sing with clarity.

CONSONANTS AND MUSICAL RHYTHM

Two things are necessary to sing vocal music with good rhythm: You must be able to read accurately the rhythmic figures contained in the music notation, and you must be able to place the proper consonant in its correct location. The following information will acquaint you with the different types of consonants, but you will further enhance your singing if you will make a conscious effort to coordinate the musical beat with the singing of a particular consonant.

You will notice that there are voiced and voiceless consonants in the following groups, and you should learn to identify the sounds contained in each category.

Lip (Labial) Consonants

Written:	*b*	*p*	*m*	*w*	*wh*[1]
	b	p	m	w	hw[2]
IPA:	[b]	[p]	[m]	[w]	[ʍ]

These and other consonants are found before, between, and after vowels, and the singing of them should be looked on as interrupting the line of vowel sounds. All consonants listed in this group are formed with the lips.

The *b* sound is voiced and the *p* sound is voiceless,[3] but the same lip action is used to produce the two consonants. Your lips are closed normally and naturally, and the consonant sound occurs at the moment of implosion. You may want to think of your lips as being pushed apart by the consonant.

The *b* sound uses the pitch of its following vowel when it is the initial consonant, and it uses the pitch of its preceding vowel when it is in the medial or final position. Such the *p* is a voiceless consonant, there is no pitch involved.

The *w* sound is voiced, and the *wh* sound is voiceless; your lips should be rounded easily forward for both sounds. The *wh* sound is always connected in the forward direction (it is connected to the previous sound). The *w* sound is connected in the forward direction when it is the first sound of a musical phrase (it is sounded

---

[1]Madeleine Marshall, *The Singer's Manual of English Diction* (New York: G. Schirmer, Inc., 1953), p. 105. "It is interesting to note that in early English, words now spelled with *wh* were spelled with *hw* (*hwen, hwat,* etc.)."

[2]The Webster symbol is listed above the IPA symbol in all charts.

[3]A voiceless consonant involves the blowing of air without vocalized sound, and a voiced consonant involves vocalized sound without the blowing of air.

early), and it is connected to the vowel sound that follows when it is in a medial or final position.

The *m* sound is voiced, and it can be thought of as being a prolonged hum (you may also wish to think of a prolonged hum as producing the *m* sound). The *m* is sung with very relaxed lips as they touch lightly. It should be connected both forward (to the preceding sound) and backward (to the succeeding sound) to give more time for the *m* to be heard. Your lips move from the *m* immediately to the vowel that follows, and you use the same pitch as is given to the vowel. The *m* sound is sung on the pitch of the preceding vowel when it is in a medial or final position.

WORDS TO SPEAK ALOUD

beauty abide pin up warm way what which mean mouth

Consonants Using the Lower Lip and Upper Teeth

Written:	*f*	*v*
	f	v
IPA:	[f]	[v]

The *v* sound is voiced, and the *f* sound is voiceless; they are articulated in the same place and in the same way. They are sounded by placing your lower lip outside of and over the tips of your front teeth. This contact results in a partial implosion as the outward flow of air is partly impeded.

The *v* sound is sung on the pitch of the subsequent vowel when it is in the initial position. When the *v* sound is added at the end of a word or phrase, your sung tone must be stopped before your lip is moved away from your upper teeth. An unwanted vowel sound will result after the consonant if you do not stop your sung tone quickly enough. The *v* sound assumes the pitch of the preceding vowel, and the *f* sound is sung as late as possible. For example, sing *a-fter,* not *af-ter,* and sing *if thou* as *i-fthou.*

WORDS TO SPEAK ALOUD

lift fall uplift for food vow vast voice laugh of

Consonants Using the Tongue and Upper Gum or Teeth

Written:	*th*	*t*	*d*	*n*	*l*	*s*	*z*	*sh*	*r*	*j*	*ch*
	th/th	t	d	n	l	s/zh	z	sh	r	j	ch
IPA:	[ð]/[θ]	[t]	[d]	[n]	[l]	[s]/[ʒ]	[z]	[ʃ]	[r]	[dʒ]	[tʃ]

Since a large number of consonant sounds fall within this classification, it will be more advantageous to discuss the sounds individually or in groups of two.

The *th* sound may be either voiced or voiceless; for example, it is voiced in *that* (the first symbol above), and it is voiceless in *think* (the second symbol above). The *th* sound is sung by placing the tip of your tongue just outside of and slightly touching the tips of your upper front teeth.

The *t* sound is voiceless, and the *d* sound is voiced. They result from contact between the tip of your tongue and your upper gum. A pitch is sounded when the *d* is sung, but there is no pitch involved in the *t* sound. The *d* sound assumes the pitch of the following vowel when it is in the initial position, and it assumes the pitch of the preceding vowel when it is in the medial or final position.

The *n* sound is voiced. It is sung by placing the tip of your tongue loosely against your upper gum and slightly raising your soft palate. It is ordinarily prolonged, and when in the initial position, it takes the pitch of the following vowel; it is sung on the pitch of the preceding vowel when it is in the medial or final position.

The *l* sound is voiced. It is sung by allowing the tip of your tongue to touch your upper gum; the sound occurs as your tongue is flipped quickly downward, away from your gum. The *l* sound is sung on the pitch of the following vowel when it is in the initial position, and it is sung on the pitch of the preceding vowel when it is in the medial or final position.

The *z* sound is voiced, and the *s* sound (as in *sound*) is voiceless. (The voiced *z* sound is often spelled as a written *s,* but in such words as *voices* and *is,* the *s* actually takes on the sound of a *z.*) The position for singing the *s* and the *z* is the same; you point the tip of your tongue toward, but do not touch, the center of your upper front teeth. While this position is held, the *s* is sounded by emitting breath over the groove of your tongue and between your slightly parted front teeth. The *z* is sung in the same manner, but it is voiced.

The *s* is usually sung as late as possible, and when in the initial or medial position, it is connected to its following vowel. When the voiceless *s* is in the final position, the tone should be stopped before your tongue is moved.

The *z* sound is sung on the pitch of its preceding vowel when it is in the final position. When it is between two vowels or in the medial position, it is sung on the pitch of the preceding vowel but it is also connected to the next sound.

The *s* as in *pleasure* is voiced, and the *sh* sound is voiceless; they are produced by using the same mouth position. Your jaw is in a generally high position, and the tip of your tongue is pointed toward, but does not touch, the center of your upper front teeth. The sides of your tongue should lightly touch your upper side teeth, but your tongue should never be pressed tightly against your teeth. Your tongue moves from this position immediately to the position of the next consonant or vowel. The connection of the voiced *s* and voiceless *sh* sounds to preceding and succeeding sounds is essentially the same as for the *z* and voiceless *s.*

The *r* sound is usually flipped, as in Italian. An American *r* is sounded when the tip of the tongue moves upward toward the upper gum ridge, but does not touch it, and then returns to its original position.[4] It can be used in some folk songs, musical comedy, or popular songs, but it is not appropriate to use an American *r* when you sing most traditional art songs. In singing a flipped *r,* you will very quickly flip the tip of your tongue against the back ridge of your upper gum (very close to where the *d* is sounded); pitch is added as your tongue is immediately flipped away from this position to the vowel sound that follows.

The *j* sound is voiced, and the *ch* sound is voiceless; they are produced by using the same mouth position. The tip of your tongue touches the back ridge of your upper gum, and the sides of your tongue are placed against the sides of your upper teeth. Air is expelled for the *ch* when the tip of your tongue is moved away from the back ridge of your upper gum; voice is added when the *j,* or soft *g,* sound is sung. The pitch of its following vowel is taken when the *j* sound is in the initial position, and it is sung on the pitch of the preceding vowel when it is in the medial or final position.

WORDS TO SPEAK ALOUD

> *that with not do noon love soon Zion lazy sure wish vision pleasure run cry far around trouble judge church*

Consonants Using the Back of the Tongue

Written:	*k*	*g*	*ng*
	k	g	ŋ
IPA:	[k]	[g]	[ŋ]

---

[4]Marshall, *The Singer's Manual of English Diction,* p. 9.

The g and ng sounds are voiced, and the k sound is voiceless. The g and k sounds may also be classed as gutturals, whereas the ng may be called a nasal. The g and k sounds are produced by raising the back of your tongue to meet your soft palate; your tongue then moves from this position immediately to the next vowel or consonant sound. The g and k sounds are sung on the pitch of the following vowel. The ng sound is sung with the back of your tongue loosely touching your soft palate, and it is sung on the pitch of the previous vowel.

WORDS TO SPEAK ALOUD

God great give king kind come sing bring along

Other Consonants

Written:	q	y	h	x
	k	y	h	ks/gz
IPA:	[k]	[j]	[h]	[ks]/[gz]

The q is sounded as a k. But when q and u are sounded together, there is a combination of two sounds. The qu sound is a combination of the k and w sounds, in which the k is voiceless and the w is voiced.

The x should be looked on as a combination of the eh sound, the voiceless, guttural k, and the voiceless, dental s. But the written x may be pronounced differently in other situations.

The y sound is sometimes a consonant and sometimes a vowel. It is a consonant at the beginning of a syllable, and it is voiced. The y is produced by arching the middle and back of your tongue toward your hard palate and moving your tongue quickly downward before the next vowel formation. The y sound uses the pitch of the following vowel when it is in the initial position, and it is added on to the pitch of the preceding vowel sound when it is in the medial position.

The aspirate h is the last consonant sound to be discussed, but it is also one of the most important. The h sound is voiceless, and it is produced by blowing air out through your mouth. Enough breath must be used to make the h sound audible, but there must never be excessive stress. The mouth formation of the next vowel is used when the h is in the initial or medial position, and expelling the breath to sound the h is followed immediately by the next vowel sound. Also, such a word as *honest* has a silent h; in this situation, the h is seen but not pronounced.

WORDS TO SPEAK ALOUD

quiet excellent xylophone he heart holy yes yet rhythm

Remember, all consonants are to be pronounced precisely, quickly, and in coordination with the musical rhythm.

14 Diphthongs and Triphthongs

Although you are advised to emphasize the study of vowels and consonants first, texts do contain other combinations of sounds. Diphthongs also occur quite frequently in vocal music.

SIX BASIC DIPHTHONGS

A diphthong includes two different vowel sounds: The first vowel is sustained, and the second vowel is added at the very end. Since the second vowel is added quite late, some teachers and singers refer to the second vowel as a "receding" or "vanishing" vowel. When a diphthong is sung on two or more pitches, the first vowel is sustained on all notes, and the second vowel is added at the very end of the last note sung. For example, observe the following two examples taken from "Bist Du Bei Mir" ("If Thou Be Near") by J. S. Bach.

When sung on a single pitch, the second vowel sound (*oo* in this example) is added at the very end.

When sung on more than one pitch, the second vowel sound (*ih* in this example) is added at the very end of the last note sung.

"There are six recognizable diphthongs used in English, as found in 'day,' 'eye,' 'owe,' 'boy,' 'now,' 'you.' "[1] There are no diphthongs in French, but it is possible to have comparable sounds as, for example, in *travail*. There are almost no diphthongs in Italian, although there are many examples where vowels follow one another very rapidly; but even then, each vowel sound is allowed to retain its own distinct character.

Sounded as in *Eye*
Written: ī[2]
IPA: [aɪ]

[1]William Vennard, *Singing: The Mechanism and the Technic* (New York: Carl Fischer, Inc., 1967), p. 176.

[2]The Webster symbol is listed above the IPA symbol in all charts.

This diphthong is also found in the word *night;* it is made up of the sounds *ah* and *ih* (or *ee*) and is generally sounded as *ah-ih,* although some singers prefer *ah-ee.* Observe the following points when you sing this diphthong:

1. The prolonged sound is *ah,* and it should be sung as described in Unit 12. If you allow your lips to protrude too far, you will tend to sing this vowel too "dark," or too far back in your mouth. The sound will be sung properly if it is placed forward, as in *father.*
2. The second, or receding, sound should be sung as an *ih* (or *ee*) and at the very end; but it should be sounded. *Do not omit the second sound.*

WORDS TO SPEAK ALOUD

sigh mine thine high time life mind lie defy sign

Sounded as in *Day*
Written: ā
IPA: [eɪ]

This diphthong is made up of the sounds *ay* and *ih* (or *ee*) and is generally sounded as *ay-ih,* although some singers prefer *ay-ee.* Observe the following points when you sing this diphthong:

1. The prolonged sound is *ay,* although some singers may want to use an *eh* sound. If you will alternately sing an *ay* and *eh,* you may notice increased tension in your lips and/or jaw when you sing the *ay* sound. Although *ay* is the usual sound, you may find that you sing more freely when you use the *eh* sound.
2. The second vowel recedes, and it should be sung as an *ih* (or *ee*) sound.

WORDS TO SPEAK ALOUD

play lay say fate wave pray away same late

Sounded as in *Boy*
Written: ȯi
IPA: [ɔɪ]

This diphthong, also found in the word *voice,* is generally sounded as *aw-ih,* although some singers prefer *aw-ee.* Observe the following points when you sing this diphthong:

1. The *aw* is the first, the prolonged, sound. It is sung with the back of your tongue arched slightly more than for the *ah* sound; with the tip of your tongue forward and down; with your lips protruding in an oval shape; and with your lower jaw down and relaxed.
2. The second, or receding, sound is to be sung as an *ih* (or *ee*) sound.

WORDS TO SPEAK ALOUD

joy toy enjoy employ annoy destroy royal choice rejoice

Sounded as in *Now*
Written: au̇
IPA: [aʊ]

This diphthong, generally sounded as *ah-oo,* is also found in the word *about.* Although these words are spelled with an *o,* the primary vowel sound is actually an *ah* sound. Observe the following points when you sing this diphthong:

1.   The primary sound, *ah*, should be sung as discussed in Unit 12.
2.   The second, or receding, sound is *oo*.

WORDS TO SPEAK ALOUD

vow   how   thousand   shout   round   allow   bough   brow

Sounded as in *Throw*
Written: ō
IPA: [oʊ]

This diphthong, generally sounded as *oh-oo,* is also found in the word *though.* It is always important for you to identify the exact sound to be sung. If sounds are not specifically and correctly identified, a singer may substitute such unnatural sounds as *geh-oh* for *go.* In such a situation, the result will be unwanted tonal distortion. Observe the following points when you sing this diphthong:

1.   The primary, prolonged sound, the *oh,* should be sung as discussed in Unit 12.
2.   The second, or receding, sound should also be sung as discussed in Unit 12, but now the *oo* sound is placed at the very end. The positions of the tongue, lips, and jaw are the same, but the *oo* sound is now not emphasized.

WORDS TO SPEAK ALOUD

know   glow   blow   window   foe   woe   home   alone   no

Sounded as in *Few*
Written: ü
IPA: [ju]

Generally sounded as *ee-oo*—although some singers prefer *ih-oo*—this is sometimes called an inverted diphthong.[3] The prolonged sound is now the second sound, and the receding sound is now the first sound—the reverse of the preceding situations. Observe the following points when you sing this inverted diphthong:

1.   The first vowel sound, *ee* (or *ih*), should be sounded as discussed in Unit 12, but you should remember that it is now the receding sound.
2.   The second, or prolonged, vowel sound is also to be sung as discussed in Unit 12; its sound is as in *move,* not as in *look.*

WORDS TO SPEAK ALOUD

view   new   cute   hue   pew   move   beautiful   rebuke   knew

OTHER DIPHTHONGS AND TRIPHTHONGS

It would be premature to expect you, in your first months of study, to recognize every possible diphthong and triphthong. You now have information about the six most often used diphthongs; the points that follow are found less often, and they will be discussed more briefly.

In addition to the six basic diphthongs, there are others that end in a neutral vowel. As a group, these diphthongs contain one of the prolonged vowel sounds listed earlier and the neutral vowel in the second position (for example, as in *sofa*). These diphthongs also are found in such words as *fear, fair, far, for, pore,* and *poor.*

---

[3]But some teachers prefer to ask their singers to use *y-oo.*

Triphthongs contain a combination of three vowels, as in *tire* and *tower*. A triphthong has several points in common with a diphthong, but of course there are now three vowel sounds to be sung: The first vowel is sustained as in a diphthong, and the last two vowels are added at the very end. When a triphthong is sung on more than one pitch, the first vowel is sustained on all notes (as in a diphthong), and the second and third vowels are added at the very end. The essential difference is that there are now two receding vowels to be sung at the very end; for example, *our* would be sung as [aʊə].

In conclusion, you should acquaint yourself specifically with the six basic diphthongs listed first. Those diphthongs and triphthongs discussed later will also need to be understood when they appear in the music you sing, but you will meet them less often at this stage of your training. Therefore, more specific study of those diphthongs and triphthongs can be undertaken later.

15 *Pronunciation in English*

The objective of this unit is to provide a concise guide to English pronunciation. Clear, articulate, and distinct pronunciation can greatly enhance your singing, and you should consider the text to be an essential part of the music. Indeed, it is the text that sets a singer apart from an instrumentalist.

SPEAKING AND SINGING

You should begin by thinking about the relationship of singing and speaking, for singing has been called intensified speech. A clear, freely produced, resonant speaking voice can provide a solid foundation on which to build a more refined singing voice.

You may begin by giving your attention to the following points:

1. Practice reading aloud until you become an accomplished reader.
2. Approach both singing and speaking in a spontaneous manner.
3. Use a standard dictionary for correcting any mispronunciations or other inappropriate speech patterns.
4. Read the text aloud many times before you begin to sing, and always read with the same sense of communication you intend to project when you actually sing the music.
5. Always communicate textual meanings when you sing to other people.

The following pages will give you information for improving your diction; you are asked to read the instructions and speak the English words aloud.

Consonants

				IPA
r[1]	1. Usually flipped.		around	[əraund]
r	2. American *r* used in folk songs, musical comedy, or popular songs; also for *tr* and *dr* combinations (except on very high notes).		trouble	[trʌbəl]
IPA: [r]				
y	Sounded as a consonantal vowel when found at the beginning of a syllable.		you	[ju]
y				
IPA: [j]				

[1]Each letter in the left-hand column appears first in its written form, followed by the Webster and the IPA symbols.

Voiced and Voiceless Consonants[2]

			IPA
t (voiceless) *d* (voiced) t,d IPA: [t], [d]	Both sounded as a result of contact between the tip of the tongue and the upper gum.	no*t* *d*o	[nɑt] [du]
p (voiceless) *b* (voiced) p, b IPA: [p], [b]	1. Sounded as the result of contact between the lips. 2. The *b* is silent in words ending in *mb*.	slee*p* *b*a*b*y com*b*	[slip] [beɪbi] [koʊm]
f (voiceless) *v* (voiced) f, v IPA: [f], [v]	Sounded by placing the lower lip outside of and over the tips of the upper front teeth.	*f*ear *v*oice	[fiɚ][3] [vɔɪs]
k (voiceless) *g* (voiced) k, g IPA: [k], [g]	Sounded as the result of raising the back of the tongue to meet the soft palate.	wor*k* *g*o	[wɚk] [goʊ]
th (voiceless) *th* (voiced) th, *th* IPA: [θ], [ð]	Sounded by placing the tip of the tongue just outside of and slightly touching the tips of upper front teeth.	*th*ink *th*at	[θɪŋk] [ðæt]
wh (voiceless) *w* (voiced) hw, w IPA: [ʍ], [w]	1. Sounded as the *w* but with an *h* instead of the *oo* sound. 2. Started with the *oo* and immediately followed with the *w*.	*wh*ere *w*atch	[ʍɛr] [watʃ]
s (voiceless) *z* (voiced) s, z IPA: [s], [z]	1. The tip of the tongue is pointed toward (but not touching) the center of the upper front teeth. 2. Sounded as for an *s* but with voice added on the pitch given.	*s*oon la*z*y	[sun] [leɪzi]
sh (voiceless) *s* (voiced) sh, zh IPA: [ʃ], [ʒ]	1. The sides of the tongue are placed against the upper side teeth, with the tip pointed toward (but not touching) the center of the upper front teeth; air is blown for *sh*. 2. Sounded as for *sh* but with voice added (air is not blown).	*s*ure plea*s*ure vi*s*ion	[ʃɚ] [plɛʒɚ] [vɪʒən]
ch (voiceless) *j* or soft *g* (voiced) ch, j IPA: [tʃ], [dʒ]	1. The tip of the tongue touches the center of the upper gum; air is blown and the tongue is moved from the upper gum. 2. The same tongue action is used as for *ch*, but voice is added.	*ch*ange *j*ump	[tʃeɪndʒ] [dʒʌmp]
m (voiced) m	1. An initial *m* is followed by a vowel; it begins a word or syllable.	*m*ay	[meɪ]

[2]Many of the following consonants are listed in pairs. In such instances, the IPA and Webster symbols for the letter listed above appear to the left. For example, the IPA and Webster symbols for *t* appear first, and the symbols for *d* appear second.

Note: Transcription into the International Phonetic Alphabet (IPA) in Units 15 and 16 is by Ann M. Miller.

[3]The symbol [ɚ] is used for the sound of *er* as in *her*.

IPA

IPA: [m]	2. The *m* is a prolonged hum; it is sung with very relaxed lips.		
n (voiced) n IPA: [n]	1. An initial *n* is followed by a vowel; it may begin a word or a syllable. 2. The tongue loosely touches the upper gum while the soft palate is raised. 3. In most instances, the *n* is prolonged.	*n*ow *n*oo*n*	[naʊ] [nun]
l (voiced) l IPA: [l]	1. Sung by using the tip of the tongue; an initial *l* is sung as late as possible, and a final *l* is sung early. 2. The tip of the tongue touches the upper gum; it is quickly flipped downward, away from the gum.	*l*ove a*l*l	[lʌv] [ɔl]
ng (voiced) ŋ IPA: [ŋ]	Sung with the back of the tongue loosely touching the soft palate; sung on the pitch of the preceding vowel.	si*ng*	[sɪŋ]
h (voiceless)	1. A stream of air strong enough to be heard is blown. 2. It may be a silent letter.	*h*appy *h*our	[hæpi] [aʊɚ]

Vowels

ā IPA: [e]	1. The tip of the tongue should touch the lower front teeth. 2. The lips are pointed away from the teeth, and the lower jaw is lowered to a comfortable position.	take[4]	[teɪk]
ä (ah) IPA: [ɑ]	One of the most basic vowel sounds.	father	[fɑðɚ]
e (eh) IPA: [ɛ]	1. Found in various spellings. 2. Approached by lowering the lower lip to a comfortable position.	death wed said any	[dɛθ] [wɛd] [sɛd] [ɛni]
i (as in *him*) IPA: [ɪ][5]	1. Found in various spellings. 2. It is important to distinguish this sound from an *e* sound.	it guilt myth	[ɪt] [gɪlt] [mɪθ]
ē *(ee)* IPA: [i]	The back of the tongue is raised more than for the preceding vowel sounds.	see	[si]
a IPA: [æ]	1. Not be confused with the *ah* or *eh* sounds. 2. The tongue and corners of the mouth tend to be slightly wider for this sound.	bat	[bæt]
ü (oo) IPA: [u]	The lips are rounded and pointed forward in a circular fashion.	too	[tu]
* u̇* (as in *put*) IPA: [ʊ]	Formed as in the preceding *ü* but with the rounding slightly larger; the lips are not as pointed as for the *ü* in *too*.	put book	[pʊt [bʊk]

[4]Although sung as a vowel sound, it is spoken as a diphthong.
[5]Some sources use the following symbol: [i].

$\bar{o}$ IPA: [o]	1. The lips are rounded, but they are not as pointed as for the $\bar{u}$ sound. 2. The lower jaw should be loose but lower than for the $\bar{u}$ sound.	over[6]	[oʊvɚ]
$\dot{o}$ *(aw)* IPA: [ɔ]	1. The lips are rounded, but they are not as pointed as for the *oh* sound. 2. The lower jaw should be loose and in approximately the same position as for the *oh* sound.	draw	[drɔ]
u (uh) IPA: [ʌ]	Sounded only in stressed syllables and formed in the back of the mouth.	mud	[mʌd]
The neutral vowel IPA: [ə]	Never stressed and formed in the center of the mouth.	sofa	[soʊfə]

Additional information may be found in the following sources:

ADLER, KURT, *Phonetics and Diction in Singing*. Minneapolis: University of Minnesota Press, 1967.

MARSHALL, MADELEINE, *The Singer's Manual of English Diction*. New York: G. Schirmer, Inc.

PFAUTSCH, LLOYD, *English Diction for the Singer*. New York: Lawson-Gould Music Publishers, Inc., 1971.

URIS, DOROTHY, *To Sing in English*. New York: Boosey & Hawkes, Inc., 1971.

[6]Although sung as a vowel sound, it is spoken as a diphthong.

16 *Foreign Languages*

The objective of this unit is to present the basic principles of Italian, French, and German diction.

Although it is recommended that you begin by singing in your native language, there are many students who have studied a second language. Most singing students learn the basic principles of Italian, French, and German diction, and many teachers believe Italian songs are particularly important.

TRANSLATIONS

Americans traditionally have been slow to encourage the use of English translations, and there even has been some feeling that translations never can be as good as the original text. Although the English language does often present problems, there now is increasing support for singing texts in one's native tongue. In fact, if a singer's purpose is to communicate, it is all-important for the performers themselves to comprehend exactly what they are singing. In *The NATS Bulletin* a few years ago, a president's editorial urged the wider use of English in American performance: "Everywhere there is verbal license to perform translations, their use seems to answer a practical need, and yet there remains a reluctance to use them."[1]

That reluctance may be caused by the fact that good, singable translations are hard to find. Too often, translators have not been careful enough about the relationship of the music to the words. But such unsatisfactory experiences should not stop English-speaking singers from continuing to search for successful translations.

You should ask yourself the following questions before you make a decision about whether you should sing a particular text in translation.

1. *Does the translation essentially preserve the original rhythmic relationship of the text and music?* There should be no awkward or misplaced rhythmic accents in the translation.
2. *Does the translation preserve the spirit and essential meaning of the original text?* It is generally not expected that the exact meanings of the original words will be retained in the translation, but essentially the same meanings should be present in both the translation and the original text.
3. *Does the translation have an easy flow of consonant and vowel sounds as you speak the text aloud?*
4. *Do the vowels assigned to the highest or lowest pitches allow you to sing those sounds naturally and easily?*

Some texts are so carefully set in the original language that they cannot be translated successfully, and there are times when it is best to sing a text in the original language:

---

[1]Quoted from an earlier *Bulletin* by Charles W. Chapman, "Words, Music, and Translations," *The NATS Bulletin* (October 1977), p. 22.

1. When you sing for an audience that will understand the text in the original language
2. When you sing in a competition or for an audition, where you are expected to sing music in the original language
3. When no desirable translation exists for the music you are to sing or when you simply choose to use the original text

The following principles will provide the basic information you need to begin singing in Italian, French, and German. The sources listed in the footnotes also can be a great help.

ITALIAN

Vowels[2]

Front Vowels	Back Vowels
i	u
e	o
ɛ	ɔ

a

Low Vowel

			IPA
a IPA: [ɑ:]	Sounded as *ah.*	a̲ma	[ɑ:mɑ][3]
e IPA: [e], [ɛ:][4]	Sounded as *ay* in *take,* or as *eh* in *met.*	padre̲ me̲nza	[pɑ:dre] [mɛ:ntzɑ]
i IPA: [i:]	Sounded as *ee* in *machine.*	si̲	[si:]
o IPA: [o:], [ɔ]	Sounded as *oh* in *hope,* or as *aw* in *off.*	mi̲o Ro̲dolfo	[mio] [rɔdolfo][5]
u IPA: [u:]	Sounded as *oo* in *noon.*	tu̲	[tu:]

Consonants

b IPA: [b]	Sounded as a voiced *b* in English.	b̲allo	[bɑ:llo]
c IPA: [k], [tʃ]	1. Sounded as *k* (but nonaspirated) before *a, o, u, l,* or *r.* 2. Similar to a *ch* sound when before *e* and *i.*	c̲arro c̲ielo	[kɑ:rro] [tʃɛ:lo]
d IPA: [d]	Sounded with the tip of the tongue lightly touching the back of the front teeth.	d̲uro	[du:ro]
f IPA: [f]	Sounded approximately as in English.	f̲elice	[feli:tʃe]

[2]This chart appears in Evelina Colorni, *Singers' Italian* (New York: Schirmer Books, 1970), p. 11. On page 23 the author states: "With all Italian vowels, front, back and low, one should have a sensation of forward resonance. . . . Keeping the tip of the tongue in contact with the lower teeth will help to develop this forward sensation."

[3]This sign (:) means that the sound represented by the preceding letter is long; it is not used in some sources.

[4]When two individual sounds are listed (as *ay* and *eh* here), the IPA symbol to the left is for the sound listed first.

[5]Added time required for singing a double consonant is taken from the preceding vowel.

IPA

g (or *gh*) IPA: [g], [dʒ]	1. Sounded as a hard consonant (as in *go*) before *a, o, u* and consonants except *l* and *n*.	grande	[grɑ:ndə]
	2. Sounded as a soft *j* sound before *e* and *i*.	giro	[dʒi:ro]
h	Never pronounced.		
l IPA: [l]	Sounded with the tip of the tongue lightly touching the back of the front teeth.	lento	[lɛ:nto]
m IPA: [m]	Sounded approximately as in English.	meno	[me:no]
n IPA: [n]	Sounded with the tip of the tongue lightly touching the back of the front teeth.	nome	[no:me]
p IPA: [p]	Sounded similar to English but non-aspirated.	padre	[pɑ:dre]
qu IPA: [kw]	Sounded as in *quality;* q is found only in combination with *u.*	questo	[kwe:sto]
r IPA: [r]	Sounded more forward than for speaking; produced by the tip of the tongue moving up and down (one or more times) against the top of the upper front teeth (where the gum ridge begins).	porta	[pɔ:rtɑ]
s IPA: [s], [z]	Sounded as in *sit* or *rosy* (the *z* is voiced throughout).	servo prosa	[se:rvo] [pro:zɑ]
t IPA: [t]	Sounded with the tip of the tongue lightly touching the back of the front teeth (but nonaspirated), and not as the *t* in *nation.*	terra	[tɛrrɑ]
v IPA: [v]	Sounded as in English.	veggo	[veggɔ]
z IPA: [ts], [dz]	Sounded similar to *ts* in *cats* or the *dz* sound in *beds.*	mezzo	[mɛ:dzo]

Combinations

cia, cio, ciu IPA: [tʃɑ], [tʃo], [tʃu]	Sounded similar to the *ch* in *choose* plus the vowel sound.	marcia bacio fanciulla	[mɑ:rtʃɑ] [bɑ:tʃo] [fantʃu:llɑ]
che, chi IPA: [ke], [ki]	Sounded as *k* plus the vowel sound.	marche chiesa	[mɑ:rke] [kie:zɑ]
sca, sco, scu IPA: [skɑ], [sko], [sku]	Sounded as *ska, sko,* and *sku.*	scatola scoperta scuola	[skɑto:lɑ] [skopɛ:rtɑ] [skuo:la]
scia, scio, sciu IPA: [ʃɑ], [ʃo], [ʃu]	Sounded as *sha, sho, shu.*	sciabola sciopero sciutto	[ʃabo:lɑ] [ʃopɛ:ro] [ʃu:tto]
sche, schi IPA: [skɛ], [ski]	Sounded as *ske* and *ski.*	scherma Schicchi	[skɛ:rmɑ] [ski:kki]

			IPA
gia, gio, giu IPA: [dʒa], [dʒo], [dʒu]	Sounded similar to the *j* in *jar* plus the vowel sound.	*gia*ccio *Gio*vanni *Giu*gno	[dʒattʃɔ] [dʒovaːnni] [dʒuːɲo]
ghe, ghi IPA: [gɛ], [gi]	Sounded as *g* in *go* plus the vowel sound.	Mar*ghe*rita a*ghi*	[marɡɛriːta] [aːgi]
sga, sgo, sgu IPA: [sga], [sgo], [sgu]	Sounded similar to *zg* plus the vowel sound.	*sga*bello *sgo*mento *sgu*ardo	[sgabɛːllo] [sgomɛːnto] [sgwaːrdo]
sghe, sghi IPA: [sgɛ], [sgi]	Sounded similar to *zg* plus the vowel sound.	*sghe*rro *sghi*gno	[sgɛːrro] [sgiːɲo]
gn IPA: [ɲ]	Sounded as the *ni* in *pinion*.	monta*gna*	[montaːɲa]

FRENCH

Often, the most difficult adjustment is to the French nasal vowels, for which there is no English counterpart. However, the following quotation clearly describes how to sing these sounds:

> A "nasal" vowel is correctly resonated in the nasal cavities which are located behind the nose, in the "yawn," more or less in the center of the head. It must *never* be placed solely in the nose! A correctly resonated nasal vowel-sound has added richness and depth. This is achieved when one-third of the vocalic flow is allowed to resonate in the nasal cavities, right above the soft palate and behind the nose. The soft palate is gently dropped in the process, thus permitting entry into these resonating chambers in the center of the head. The process has often been compared to 'covering the tone'. . . . The major part of the vocalic flow, however, must continue to emanate from the mouth.[6]

French nasal vowels are shown on the following pages by the use of a ~ above the particular letter or sound symbol. For example, see the IPA symbols for *errant* [ɛrɑ̃].

	Vowels		IPA
a (or *à*) IPA: [a], [ɑ̃]	1. Usually sounded as in *watch* or a little broader. 2. Sounded as *ah* when before a final *s*. 3. Sounded as [ɑ̃] (nasalized when followed by *m* or *n*).	*a*mi err*a*nt	[ami] [ɛrɑ̃][7]
â (circumflex) IPA: [ɑ]	Usually sounded as *ah*.	ch*â*teau	[ʃato]
ai or (or *aî*) IPA: [ɛ], [ɛ̃]	1. Usually an *eh* sound as in *met*. 2. Sounded as [ɛ̃] when followed by *m* or *n*.	pl*ai*re air*ai*n	[plɛːr][8] [ɛrɛ̃]
au IPA: [o]	Usually sounded as *oh*.	*au*ssi be*au*coup	[osi] [bokʊ]

---

[6]Thomas Grubb, *Singing in French: A Manual of French Diction and French Vocal Repertoire* (New York: Schirmer Books, 1979), pp. 54–55.

[7]This *r* [r] is used when singing, but the uvular *r* [R] is used when speaking.

[8]This sign(ː) means that the sound represented by the preceding letter is long; it is not used in some sources.

			IPA
e IPA: [ε], [ə]	1. Sounded as *eh* when followed by a double consonant.	cachette	[kaʃɛt]
	2. Otherwise sounded as *uh,* or silent when final.	pleine	[plɛn]
é (acute) IPA: [e]	Sounded as ā.	école	[ekɔl]
è (grave) IPA: [ε]	Sounded as in *set*.	guère	[gɛːr]
ê circumflex IPA: [ε]	Sounded as in *set*.	rêver	[rɛve]
eau IPA: [o]	Sounded as *oh*.	chapeau	[ʃapo]
ei IPA: [ε], [ɛ̃]	1. Usually sounded as *ehy*.	réveil	[revɛːj]
	2. Sounded as [ɛ̃] when followed by *m* or *n*.	rein	[rɛ̃]
eu IPA: [œː], [ø]	1. Usually sounded as *e* in *her*.	peur	[pœːr]
	2. Sometimes sounded as [ø].	peu	[pø]
i IPA: [iː], [j], [ɛ̃]	1. Usually sounded as *e* in *bee*.	ici	[iːsiː]
	2. Often sounded as *y* when preceding another vowel.	facial	[fasjal]
	3. Sounded as [ɛ̃] (nasalized when followed by *m* or *n*).	matin	[matɛ̃]
il IPA: [j]	Sounded as *y* after a vowel.	conseil	[kõsɛːj]
o IPA: [ɔ], [o], [õ]	1. May be sounded as *aw*.	ordinaire	[ɔrdinɛr]
	2. Sounded as *oh* when the final sound of a word.	nos	[no]
	3. Usually sounded as *oh* when before an *s.*	rosier	[rozje]
	4. Sounded as [õ] (nasalized when followed by *m* or *n*).		
ô (circumflex) IPA: [o]	Sounded as *oh*.	sitôt	[sito]
oeu IPA: [ø], [œ]	1. Sounded as [ø] when the last sound of a word.	voeu	[vø]
	2. Otherwise sounded as [œ].	oeuf	[œf]
oi IPA: [wa], [wɛ̃]	1. Usually sounded as *wa*.	choir	[ʃwaːr]
	2. Sounded as [wɛ̃] when followed by a nasal consonant [m], [n], or [ɲ].	loin	[lwɛ̃]
ou IPA: [u], [w]	1. Usually sounded as *oo*.	nouveau	[nuvo]
	2. Sounded similar to a *w* when before another vowel.	oui	[wi]
u IPA: [y], [ɥ], [œ̃]	1. Usually sounded as [y].	ruban	[rybɑ̃]
	2. Sounded as [ɥ] before another vowel.	nuages	[nɥaːʒ]
	3. Sounded as [œ̃] (nasalized when followed by *m* or *n*).	humble	[œ̃ːbl]
	4. Usually sounded as *uh* when in a final *um.*		
	5. Silent after *g* or *q*.	quand	[kɑ̃]

	Consonants		*IPA*
b IPA: [b], [p]	1. Usually sounded as in English. 2. Sounded as *p* when before a *c, s,* or *t.*	ha*b*itant a*b*sent	[abitã] [ɑpsã]
c IPA: [s], [k]	1. Sounded as *s* before *i* or *e.* 2. Otherwise sounded as *k* or is silent.	*c*elle *c*oin	[sɛl] [kwɛ̃]
ç (cedilla) IPA: [s]	Sounded as *s.*	gar*ç*on	[garsõ]
ch IPA: [ʃ], [k]	1. Usually sounded as *sh.* 2. Otherwise sounded as *k.*	*ch*iche *ch*oeur	[ʃiʃ] [kœ:r]
d IPA: [d], [t]	1. Usually sounded as in English. 2. Sounded as *t* when linked.	*d*étacher pren*d*-il	[detaʃe] [prãtil]
f IPA: [f], [v]	1. Sounded as in English. 2. Sometimes linked as a *v.*	*f*ermer neu*f*ans	[fɛrme] [nœvã]
g IPA: [g], [ʒ], [k]	1. Usually sounded as in English. 2. Sounded as *zh* before *i* or *e.* 3. Rarely sounded, when linked, as *k.*	*g*loire a*g*ir	[glwa:r] [aʒi:r]
gn IPA: [ɲ]	Usually sounded as *ny.*	rè*gn*e	[rɛɲ]
h IPA: [h]	Usually silent.	*h*éroine	[erɔin]
j IPA: [ʒ]	Sounded as *zh.*	*j*e	[ʒə]
k IPA: [k]	Sounded as in English.	*k*épi	[kepi]
l IPA: [l]	Usually sounded similar to an *l* in English.	*l*a	[la]
m IPA: [m]	1. Usually sounded as in English. 2. Silent when before another consonant (serves only to make the preceding vowel nasal).	*m*ille tro*m*pette	[mil] [trõpɛt]
n IPA: (unsounded), [n]	1. Silent when final or before another consonant; serves only to make the preceding vowel nasal. 2. Otherwise usually sounded as in English.	mama*n* te*n*ant	[mamã] [tənã]
p IPA: [p]	Sounded as in English.	*p*arole	[parɔl]
ph IPA: [f]	Sounded as an *f.*	*ph*are	[fa:r]
q (or *qu*] IPA: [k]	Sounded as a *k.*	cin*q*	[sɛ̃:k]
r IPA: [r]	Sung by using the tongue (not the uvular *r*).	*r*iste	[trist]
s IPA: [s], [z]	1. Usually sounded as in English. 2. Sounded as a *z* when between two vowels or when linked.	*s*avez dé*s*irer	[save] [dezire]

			IPA
ss IPA: [s]	Sounded as a single *s*.	fosse	[fo:s]
t IPA: [t]	1. Usually sounded as in English. 2. Sounded as *s* in terminations having *ti* followed by a vowel (except in *sti*).	table nation	[tabl] [nasjõ]
th IPA: [t]	Sounded as a *t*.	thé	[te]
v IPA: [v]	Sounded as in English.	vers	[vɛ:r]
w IPA: [v]	Seldom seen in French, but sounds as a *v*.	Walkyrie	[valkiri]
x IPA: [k], [ks], [gz], [z]	1. Sounded as a *k* before *ce* or *ci*. 2. Sounded as *ks* when before another consonant. 3. Sounded as *gz* after an *e* and preceding a vowel. 4. Sounded as *z* when linked.	excellent exprimer exalter dix-années	[ɛksɛlã] [ɛksprime] [ɛgzalte] [dizane]
y IPA: [j], [i]	1. Usually sounded as in English when before a vowel. 2. Otherwise sounded as an *e*.	yeux pays	*[jœ]* [pɛi]
z IPA: [z]	Sounded as in English.	gazette	[gazɛt]

Additional information may be found in the following sources:

DOUGLAS, J. H., and others, comp., *Cassell's Concise French-English English-French Dictionary*. New York: Macmillan, 1968.

GRUBB, THOMAS, *Singing in French: A Manual of French Diction and French Vocal Repertoire*. New York: Schrimer Books, 1979.

MANSION, J. E., ed., *Mansion's Shorter French and English Dictionary*. Lexington, Mass.: Heath, n.d.

GERMAN

An umlaut (··) is often used in German, and there are no English counterparts to such sounds. But in each instance, the IPA symbols included on the right side of the page will serve as your best guide to the particular sound desired.

Vowels and Diphthongs

			IPA
a IPA: [a:]	Sounded as in the *ah* in *father*.	Vater	[fɑ:tɚ][9]
ä (or ae) IPA: [e], [ɛ]	1. Sounded as *ā* before an *h* and before a single consonant. 2. Otherwise sounded as *eh*.	ähnlich ändern	[enlıç] [ɛndɚn]
ai IPA: [ɑɪ]	Sounded as *igh* in *sigh*.	Mai	[maɪ]
au IPA: [aʊ]	Sounded as *ow* in how.	Hauch	[haʊx]

[9]This sign (:) means the sound represented by the preceding letter is long; it is not used in some sources. The [ɚ] symbol is used for the sound *er* as in *her*.

			IPA
äu IPA: [ɔɪ]	Sounded as *oy* in *toy*.	Käufer	[kɔɪfəʳ]
e IPA: [ə], [ɛ], [e]	1. Sounded as *uh* when final and in the initial syllables *be-* and *ge-*.	Liebe	[li:pə]
	2. Sounded as *uh* in inflectional endings except *e*, and in unstressed noninitial syllables.	Nebel	[nebəl]
	3. Sounded as *eh* in prefixes, except in *be-* and *ge-*.	Erlauben	[ɛrlaʊbən]
	4. Sounded as *ā* in accented syllables, before *h*, before a single consonant, and when doubled.	Jeder	[jedəʳ]
	5. Sounded as *eh* in accented syllables when followed by two consonants.	Eltern	[ɛltəʳn]
ei IPA: [aɪ]	Sounded as *igh* in *sigh*.	Ein	[aɪn]
eu IPA: [ɔɪ]	Sounded as *oy* in *toy*.	Feurig	[fɔɪrɪç]
i IPA: [ɪ], [i]	1. Usually sounded as in *fit*. 2. Sounded as *e* before *h* and in *dir, lid, mir, wir*, and *wider*.	immer wider	[ɪməʳ] [vi:dəʳ]
ie IPA: [i]	Usually sounded as *e*.	lieber	[li:bəʳ]
o IPA: [o], [ɔ]	1. Sounded as *o* before a single consonant, or before *h* when final or doubled.	rot	[ro:t]
	2. Otherwise usually sounded similar to *aw*.	Gott	[gɔt]
ö (or *oe*) IPA: [ø], [œ]	1. Sounded as in *urn* before *h* or before a single consonant.	Höhe	[hø:ə]
	2. Otherwise sounded as [œ].	öffnet	[œ:fnət]
u IPA: [u], [ʊ], [v]	1. Sounded as *oo* before *h* and before a single consonant.	Blume	[blu:mə]
	2. Otherwise usually sounded as [ʊ].	Mutter	[mʊtəʳ]
	3. Sounded as *v* after the letter *q*.	erquickend	[ɛrkvɪkənt]
ü (or *ue*) IPA: [y]	1. Sounded as [y] before *h* and before a single consonant.	glühen	[glyən]

Consonants

b IPA: [b], [p]	1. Sounded as in English when beginning a word or syllable.	Leben	[le:bən]
	2. Sounded as *p* when the last letter of a word, before a voiceless consonant, or in the prefix *ab*.	Stab	[ʃtɑp]
c IPA: [ts], [k]	1. Sounded as *ts* before *e* and *i*. 2. Otherwise sounded as *k*.	Citrone Camin	[tsɪtro:nə] [kɑmi:n]
ch IPA: [x], [k], [ç]	1. Sounded forward (*ich*) or back (*ach*).	ach	[ax]

			IPA
	2. Sounded as *k* when before *a, o, l,* or *r.*	*Ch*rist	[krist]
	3. Sounded as [ç] in the *ich* ending.	ähn*lich*	[enlıç]
ck IPA: [k]	Sounded as *k*.	schre*ck*en	[ʃrɛkən]
d IPA: [d], [t]	1. Sounded as in English when beginning a word or syllable.	*D*erb	[dɛrp]
	2. Sounded as *t* when the last letter of a word or before a voiceless consonant.	Ban*d*	[bɑnt]
f IPA: [f]	Sounded as in English.	Kä*f*er	[ke:fɚ]
g IPA: [ç], [k], [g]	1. Sounded as [ç] in the *ig* ending.	Köni*g*	[kø:nıç]
	2. Sounded as *k* when final or before a consonant (except in the *ig* ending).	klu*g*	[klu:k]
	3. Otherwise sounded as in English.	ge*g*en	ge:gən]
h IPA: [h]	1. Sounded as in English but silent when final or before a consonant.	*H*exe	[hɛksə]
	2. Silent after a vowel in a syllable; makes the vowel long.	ge*h*en	[ge:ən]
j IPA: [j]	Sounded as *y* in English.	*j*a	[ja:]
k IPA: [k]	Sounded as in English.	*K*raft	[kraft]
l IPA: [l]	Sounded as in English.	*L*ieb	[li:p]
m IPA: [m]	Sounded as in English.	*m*ehr	[me:ɚ]
n IPA: [n]	Sounded as in English but like *ng* before *k*.	sche*n*ken	[ʃɛŋkən]
ng IPA: [ŋ]	Sounded as *ng* in *sing*.	Fi*ng*er	[fıŋɚ]
p IPA: [p]	Sounded as in English.	A*p*fel	[ɑpfəl]
q IPA: [k]	Sounded as *k* in English.	*Q*uell	[kvɛl]
r IPA: [r]	Sounded as an English *r* said with the tongue.	*r*ot	[rot]
s IPA: [s], [z], [ʃ]	1. Sounded as in English when doubled, when between a voiceless consonant and a following vowel, and when final.	be*ss*er	[bɛsɚ]
	2. Sounded as *z* before a vowel at the beginning of a word, between vowels, and between a voiced consonant and a following vowel.	Na*s*e	[nɑ:zə]
	3. Sounded as *sh* before *p* or *t* at the beginning of a word.	*S*piele	[ʃpilə]

				IPA
sch IPA: [ʃ]	Sounded as *sh* in English.	*Sch*nee		[ʃneː]
sp IPA: [ʃ]	Sounded as *sh* in English.			
t IPA: [ts], [t]	1. Sounded as *ts* before an *i* that is followed by another vowel. 2. Usually sounded as in English.	Na*t*ion *T*al		[natsion] [taːl]
th IPA: [t]	Sounded as *t* in English.			
v IPA: [f]	1. Usually sounded as *f* in English. 2. May sound as *v* in English.	*V*ater *Kl*avier		[faːtɚ] [klɑviːɚ]
w IPA: [v]	Sounded as *v* in English.	*w*as		[vɑːs]
x IPA: [ks]	Sounded as *ks* in English.	He*x*e		[hɛksə]
y IPA: [i]	Usually sounded as *e* in English.	C*y*presse		[tsiprɛːsə]
z IPA: [ts]	Sounded as *ts* in English.	*z*u		[tsu]

Additional information may be found in the following sources:

BETTERIDGE, HAROLD T., ed., *The New Cassell's German Dictionary*. New York: Funk & Wagnalls Co., 1958.

COX, RICHARD G., *The Singer's Manual of German and French Diction*. New York: Schirmer Books, 1970.

ODOM, WILLIAM, *German for Singers*. New York: Schirmer Books, 1981.

17 *Studio and Public Appearances*

Most opportunities to perform are offered after a student has studied for some time, but you may be offered some invitations in your first year or two of study. Thus, it will always be helpful for you to know the usual performance conditions before you are asked to sing for an audience.

Your first step in learning what will be expected of you in a performance is to attend performances of more experienced singers. Although you may want to present yourself as an individual, there are established, generally accepted standards to be observed by a singer. If you do not now anticipate your first public appearance with pleasure, you will be well advised first to review the information in Unit 3. The topics to be discussed here concern the various aspects of public performance that concern the student who is now ready to perform on stage.

INTERPRETATION OF SOLO SONGS

You have been working with solo songs for some time now, but there are other significant considerations when you sing for an audience. You will find that some aifferences exist even if your first "public" performance is simply singing for other students in the same studio where you regularly take your lessons. All singers must adjust certain aspects of their art when they first perform for a group of people; in fact, the adjustments continue as long as the singers perform. But an experienced performer, including yourself after you have studied longer, will increasingly make those adjustments automatically.

The following points are pertinent particularly to solo singers, but choral singers will also improve their art if they study privately and sing individually. Of course, a solo singer is alone responsible for communicating with an audience, whereas the conductor is responsible for integrating choral singers for a unified choral sound. However, a choral singer will be more responsive to the wishes of the conductor if that singer has also had experience in singing solo repertoire. It is expected that a choral singer who has sung individually, either privately or publicly, will be a more valuable choir member because of having had the advantage of a greater variety of singing experiences.

Adjustments must be made when you sing in public, which requires more voice, greater dynamic change, larger gestures, more eye contact with the audience, more distinct diction, and broader communication of the text and music. Of course, any technical problems associated with a particular composition should be mastered before you sing it in public; then you can place your emphasis on communicating the music to your audience. When you sing for an audience of experienced musicians, this communication may in fact take the form of a dialogue between performer and audience.

Many choral conductors do not ask their choirs to memorize music for performance, but there is real reason for a solo singer to do so. Whereas an audience may divide its attention several ways during a choral performance, all attention is focused on a solo singer.

STAGE PRESENCE

Your objective should be to maintain an unaffected, natural stage presence. If you are shy or if you have unusual stage fright, you may have difficulty in feeling natural when you sing for an audience. The essential point is to give more thought to communicating with your audience and less thought to your own feelings. If you are too concerned about how you are being accepted by an audience, you may portray a sense of inadequacy. But if you can turn your own nervousness into a feeling of excitement, you will communicate well and will portray a sense of natural enjoyment that can be understood by any audience.

You should usually dress informally for your first public performances. A man's dark business suit is accepted in most places, and a street-length dress is generally acceptable for women. Your dress may be even less formal when you sing in a studio recital. Obviously, if you sing for a formal occasion, you will generally wear formal evening dress, but that would be an exception for a singer at this stage of development.

Standards of dress change with the times and locations, and it is wise to attend similar occasions before your own public appearance is to occur.

The following points are recommended by the American Academy of Teachers of Singing; although they are intended for the mature singer, several of the points are applicable as well to young singer.[1]

Every public appearance carries with it a definite responsibility in stage deportment. Simplicity and ease of manner are the prime objectives, for these will help to bring about the poise necessary for a successful performance.

a. Remember, the singer is seen before he is heard. Walk to the place on the stage where you are to perform. Avoid extremes, such as running, dawdling, too long steps, . . . etc. Go directly and naturally to the place on the stage where you are to perform. Do not stop to bow on the way; do not bow while walking. Reach your destination and then bow.

b. A woman . . . precedes a man in going on the stage or leaving it.[2]

c. When recalled to the stage for a bow after a performance, go nearly to the place you occupied on the stage when performing, then bow at least twice before leaving that place. It is insufficient to walk a few steps onto the stage, bow once, and leave.

d. What to do with the hands is sometimes a problem. While no set rule is applicable to everyone, a few suggestions might be helpful.
—Hands and arms should drop loosely from the shoulders. They should not be held behind the body.
—Avoid making the hands conspicuous.
—If the hands touch, avoid any form of abnormal tension.
—A practice of casually holding a book of words or even a folded piece of paper loosely between the fingers is followed by some singers in order to add to their poise and self-control.

BUILDING A PROGRAM

Although few singers give solo recitals during their early months of study, it is not too soon to become acquainted with the principles involved in building a program.

[1]Permission to publish was granted by Earl Rogers, publications officer of the American Academy of Teachers of Singing.

[2]This traditional custom is not so strictly followed today.

The conductor assumes this responsibility for a choral performance, and for a more comprehensive discussion of this aspect, read "Public Performance: Matching Performers and Audience."[3]

You should first understand that considerable time, thought, and study are required to put together a program of vocal music. Since you will be the one to sing the program, it is most important for you to feel comfortable with the music selected. Beyond that point, there are generally accepted guidelines to ensure unity, variety, and proportion and to assess the total impact. Consider the following points:

1. A recital is normally divided into several groups of songs, arias, or both; each composition within a group is generally chosen from the same period of music, or there is some other unifying element. Each group of songs usually begins with a composition calculated to be both a good first song for the performer and a song that will immediately gain the undivided attention of the audience.

2. Variety is necessary, but you must normally know something of the taste of an audience before determining just how much variety will be desirable. In most situations, you will be well advised to consider such musical elements as mood, key, tempo, and dynamics. Also, you should recognize that songs are often located in a program according to their anticipated impact on an audience. Even at this stage of your singing career, you should realize that people come to listen to you sing for a great variety of reasons, which often range from being particularly interested in you as a person, singer, or musician to having a "show me what you can do" attitude. Most people in your audience will have an interest somewhere between those two extremes.

3. You will tend to achieve a more balanced sense of proportion if you first choose the first and last songs of each group. All music is important, but some people in your audience will tend to look on the intermediate compositions as leading from the first to the last songs; those people will tend to "listen with different ears" to music programmed at various positions within each group.

The first song sets the tone for the recital; it is chosen as the first composition because you are particularly comfortable in singing that particular music and because it serves better than most other compositions in creating an atmosphere of close communication between you and the audience.

The last song of a group is normally chosen because it is the music in which you find the greatest emotional and musical peak. The last composition should also be expected to be particularly pleasing to the audience.

4. It is possible to give considerable attention to the first three points and still not always have a well-chosen recital program. Therefore, it is most important to look at the total impact expected from all the music. This point is particularly important to you when you are preparing to sing a full recital. When you are choosing four, five, or six groups of songs to perform in one recital, you should first give your attention to the total structure of the program; then you should choose specific music for each portion of the program; and finally, you should look at the total impact of the actual music chosen. It takes experience to be able to judge the total impact, experience you can begin to gain by learning the reactions of your friends and fellow students. It is important to recognize that program building is an art, not a science. Because more experienced performers will have already learned some of the finer points of the art, you would be wise to study the principles they have used in choosing their programs.

The preceding four points are important when you are determining a specific order of music to sing on a full recital program. But there are several more general principles that you should also consider.[4]

[3]Kenneth E. Miller, *Handbook of Choral Music Selection, Score Preparation and Writing* (West Nyack, N.Y.: Parker Publishing Co., Inc., 1979), pp. 65–82.

[4]Information may also be found in Shirlee Emmons and Stanley Sonntag, *The Art of the Song Recital* (New York: Schirmer Books, 1979), pp. 23–79.

1. *Do not "sing down" to an audience.* Although you will want to choose music appropriate to a particular audience, it is also important to maintain your own musical standards. Performers who choose particular music just to cater to public taste will not be able to maintain their own interest, and the performance will often suffer. There is nothing wrong in choosing music that can reasonably be expected to please your audience if you also enjoy these compositions. But simple entertainment should not be your objective; the music you choose should also give your audience an opportunity to experience something of a new level of music appreciation. The elevation of musical taste occurs because people have been exposed to better music; and singers can join the ranks of those musicians who are interested in elevating public taste, just as they are interested in having their own performances well received by a particular audience.

2. *You should generally not expect to sing encores.* It is better to put all your attention into preparing the program chosen; your audience should not expect an encore of a young singer.

3. *Do not choose music that is technically more difficult than you can comfortably sing.* There is some added stress in any public performance, and it is vitally important for you to know, when you step on the stage, that you are capable of singing well every composition programmed.

4. *Although there are many ways to build a recital program, the following recommendations of the American Academy of Teachers of Singing can serve as a basis for your thinking.*[5]

(a) A group of songs of the early composers, such as Bach, Handel, Purcell, Haydn; or an entire group by early English composers; (b) a group of German Lieder by one composer or a number of composers, preferably of the Romantic school, such as Schubert, Schumann, Brahms, Strauss, Wolf; or a group of French songs by one modern style composer or a variety of composers, such as Fauré, Duparc, Chausson, Debussy, and Ravel; or a combination of both. There is also excellent material to be found in . . . acceptable English translations; (c) a carefully chosen group of modern American and/or English songs, by composers of the present or recent past; . . . and (d) a group of traditional folk-songs, authentic in their origin, and the arrangement of their accompaniment; or a second group of songs by American and/or English composers.

These four groups of songs will give ample scope to show your ability to interpret different types of music, but still this program is not normally as extensive as the one you will expect to sing after you have acquired more experience. It is important for the singer, the teacher, and the audience to remember that the first months of singing should be most of all a time for learning. If everyone approaches building a program from such a point of view, more specific considerations will tend to fall easily into a logical order.

[5]Permission to publish was granted by Earl Rogers, publications officer of the American Academy of Teachers of Singing.

18 *Vocalises*

Each of the first fifteen vocalises is written in a particular key, but you should feel free to transpose any or all of them if another key is in your best vocal range. Of course, it is expected that each of these twelve vocalises will be sung in ascending and descending keys. For example, the vocalises written in C major then should be moved up by half-steps to C-sharp major, D major, and so on, and they also should be moved down by half-steps to B major, B-flat major, and so on. The fifteen vocalises listed first are useful for all voices; those Sieber, Vaccai, and Concone vocalises listed later in the unit are appropriate for high, medium, or low ranges as identified on those pages. The vocalises should be sung on all vowels.[1]

[1]The Sieber vocalises should first be sung on vowels, but later they may be sung with the syllables included on the page.

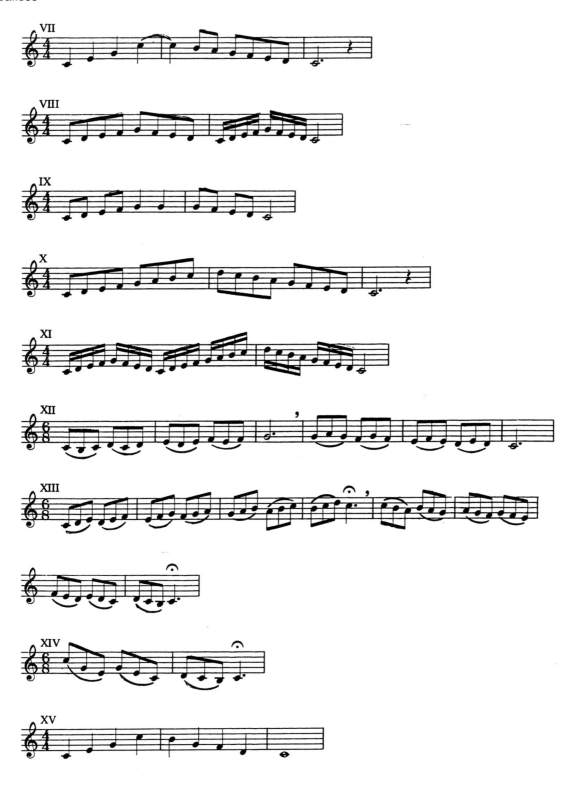

HIGH VOICE

Ferd. Sieber, Op. 92

Ferd. Sieber, Op. 92

Moderato

MEDIUM VOICE

Ferd. Sieber, Op. 93

LOW VOICE

Ferd. Sieber, Op. 96

da me ni po tu la be da me ni po tu
si do si la sol fa do re do si la sol

la be da me ni po tu la be da me
fa sol fa mi re do re sol fa la sol

ni po tu la be da me ni po
do re mi fa mi re mi fa sol

tu la be da me ni po tu la be
sol la si re do la sol fa re do

Used by permission of G. Schirmer, Inc.

da me ni po tu la be da me ni po tu la be da mi
re mi fa re fa sol la re do si la si sol fa mi

me ni po tu la be da me ni po tu la be da me ni
la do mi re la sol si la fa re si sol fa sol mi re

Concone
ed. KEM

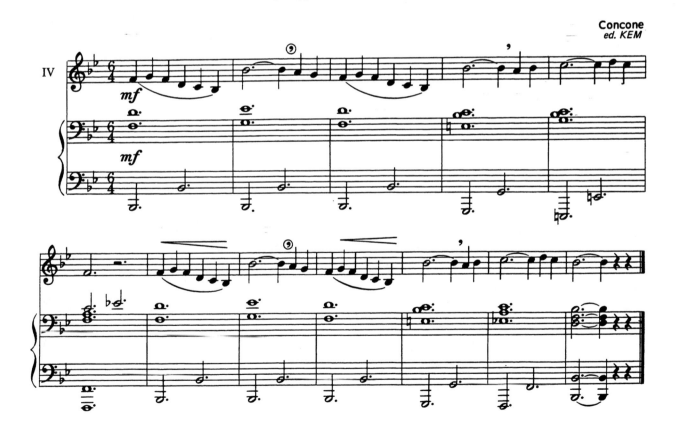

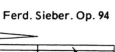

Used by permission of G. Schirmer, Inc.

98

Music for Study
and Performance

folk songs, spirituals, sacred songs, secular songs, art songs

AH, DEAREST LOVE

Caro mio ben
HIGH VOICE

Adapted from a
Translation by
James P. Dunn*

Giuseppe Giordani
(1744-1798)
ed. KEM

Larghetto

p e sostenuto

Ah, dear - est love, If you should
Ca - ro mio ben, Cre - di - mi al -

leave, When thou art far My heart is torn.___
men, Sen - za di te lan - gui - sce il cor!___

*"English Singing Translations of Foreign Language Art Songs," *National Association of Teachers of Singing*,1976. Used by permission.

Ah, dear - est love, When thou art far__ My__ heart__ is
Ca - ro mio ben, Sen - za di te__ lan - gui - sce il

torn.   Your faith-ful friend   sighs with-out
cor!   Il tuo fe - del so - spi - ra o-

end,__ This cru - el tor - ment__ cease now I pray.   This cru - el
gnor;__ Ces - sa, cru - del__ tan - to ri - gor,   Ces - sa, cru -

torment   cease now I   pray,__ cease now I pray.   Ah, dear - est
del,   tan - to ri - gor,__ tan - to ri - gor!   Ca - ro mio

AH, DEAREST LOVE

Caro mio ben

LOW VOICE

Adapted from a
Translation by
James P. Dunn*

Giuseppe Giordani
(1744 -1798)
ed. KEM

Larghetto

p e sostenuto

Ah, dear - est love, If you should leave, When thou art
Ca - ro mio ben, Cre - di - mi al - men, Sen - za di

far My heart is torn._____ Ah, dear - est
te lan - gui - sce il cor!_____ Ca - ro mio

*"English Singing Translations of Foreign Language Art Songs," *National Association of Teachers of Singing*, 1976. Used by permission.

love, When thou art far__ My__ heart__ is torn.
ben, Sen - za di te__ lan - gui - sce il cor!

Your faith - ful friend sighs with - out
Il tuo fe - del so - spi - ra o -

end, ___ This cru - el tor - ment __ cease now I
gnor; ___ Ces - sa, cru - del __ tan - to __ ri -

pray. This cru - el tor - ment cease now I
gor, Ces - sa, cru - del, tan - to ri -

ALL THROUGH THE NIGHT

HIGH VOICE

Harold Boulton

Welsh Air
ed. KEM

All through the night.
Home through the night.

Soft the drow-sy hours are creep - ing,
O'er thy spir - it gen - tly steal - ing,
Earth - ly dust from off thee shak - en,

poco accel.
p
p poco accel.

15

Hill and vale in slum - ber steep - ing
Vi - sions of de - light re - veal - ing, Breathes
Soul im - mor - tal thou shall wak - en, With

rit.
mp a tempo

I my lov - ing
a pure and
thy last dim

20

vig - il keep - ing
ho - ly feel - ing,
jour - ney tak - en,

All through the night.
Home through the night.

ALL THROUGH THE NIGHT

LOW VOICE

Harold Boulton

Welsh Air
ed. KEM

Andante

mp

p

1. Sleep, my child, and peace at-tend thee } All through the night;
2. While the moon her watch is keep-ing, } All through the night;
3. Hark! a sol-emn bell is ring-ing, Clear through the night;

Guard - ian an-gels God will send thee } All through the night,
While the wea-ry world is sleep-ing, } All through the night,
Thou, my love, art heaven-ward wing-ing, Home through the night.

Soft the drow-sy hours are creep-ing, Hill and vale in slum - ber steep-ing
O'er thy spir - it gen - tly steal-ing, Vi - sions of de - light re - veal - ing,
Earth - ly dust from off thee shak - en, Soul im - mor - tal thou shall wak - en,

I my lov - ing vig - il keep - ing } All through the night.
Breathes a pure and ho - ly feel - ing, }
With thy last dim jour - ney tak - en, Home through the night.

AMARILLI, MY DEAR ONE
Amarilli, mia bella
HIGH VOICE

Poetry by Guarini
Translation by
James P. Dunn*

Giulio Caccini
(c. 1550-1618)
ed. KEM

Adagio

A - ma - ril - li, my dear one! Doubt not my lov - ing
A - ma - ril - li, mia bel - la! Non cre - di, o, del mio

heart, You _____ most a - dor - ed, you _____ a - lone _____
cor dol - ce de - si - o: d'es - ser tu _____

_____ my be - lov - ed, Do but be - lieve, for if dark fear _____ as -
_____ l'a-mor mi - o. Cre - di - lo pur, e se ti - mor t'as - sa -

sail, Love a - lone will not fail you. Here on my
le, du - bi - tar non ti va - le. A - prim' il

*"English Singing Translations of Foreign Language Art Songs," *National Association of Teachers of Singing*, 1976. Used by permission.

bos - om see all en - grav -ed be - fore A - ma - ril - -
pet - to e ve - drai scrit - to in co - re: A - ma - ril - -

li, A - ma - ril - - li, A - ma - ril - li I a -
li, A - ma - ril - - li, A - ma - ril - li è 'l mio a -

dore you. Do but be - lieve, for if dark fear as -
mo - - re! Cre - di - lo pur, e se ti - mor t'as - sa -

sail, Love a - lone will not fail you. Here on my
le, du - bi - tar non ti va - le. A - prim' il

AMARILLI, MY DEAR ONE

Amarilli, mia bella

LOW VOICE

Poetry by Guarini
Translation by
James P. Dunn*

Giulio Caccini
(c. 1550-1618)
ed. KEM

Adagio

A - ma - ril - li, my dear one! Doubt not my lov - ing
A - ma - ril - li, mia bel - la! Non cre - di, o, del mio

heart. You ___ most a - dor - ed, you ___ a - lone ___
cor dol - ce de - si - o: d'es - ser tu

___ my be - lov - ed, Do but be - lieve, for if dark
l'a - mor mi - o. Cre - di - lo pur, e se ti -

fear ___ as - sail, Love a - lone will not fail you. Here on my
mor t'as - sa - le, du - bi - tar non ti va - le. A - prim' il

*"English Singing Translations of Foreign Language Art Songs, *National Association of Teachers of Singing*, 1976. Used by permission.

bos - om see all en - grav - ed be - fore A - ma -
pet - to e ve - drai scrit - to in co - re: A - ma -

ril - li, A - ma - ril - li, A - ma -
ril - li, A - ma - ril - li, A - ma -

ril - li, I a - dore you. Do but be - lieve, for if dark
ril - li, è'l mio a - mo - re! Cre - di - lo pur, e se ti -

fear as - sail, Love a - lone will not fail you.
mor t'as - sa - le, du - bi - tar non ti va - le.

AVE MARIA

Sir Walter Scott

Franz Schubert
(1797-1828)
ed. KEM

Note: The first verse may be repeated as a third verse.

a! | Maid - - - en - de -
a! | Un - - - de -
a! | gra - ti - a ___ ple -
a! | Ma - ter ___ De -

mild, | Oh! lis - ten to a young maid's
fil'd! | The flint - y couch where-on we're
na, | Ma - ri - a, ___ gra - ti - a -
i, | O - ra pro - no - bis pec - ca -

prayer; _____ | For Thou canst hear __ a - mid __ the
sleep - ing | Shall seem with down __ of ei - der
ple - na, | Ma - ri - a, gra - ti - a __ ple -
to - ri - bus, | O - ra, o - ra __ pro no -

wild,   'Tis __ Thou,   'tis Thou_ canst save __ a-
pil'd,   If __ Thou   a - bove_ sweet watch_ art
na,   *A -* *ve,* _____ *A -* *ve! Do - mi-*
bis,   *O -* *ra,* *o - ra* __ *pro no -*

mid _____ de-spair.   We
keep - - - - ing.   The
nus, _____ *Do - mi - nus* __ *te - cum,*   *Be - ne -*
bis _____ *pec - ca - to - ri - bus,*   *nunc*

slum - ber safe - ly till the mor - row,   Tho'
murk - y cav - ern's air so heav - y   Shall
di - cta tu in mu - li - e - ri - bus,   *et*
et in ho - ra __ *mor - tis,*   *in*

A — — ve Ma - ri — — — —
A — — ve Ma - ri — — — —
A — — *ve Ma - ri* — — — —
A — — *ve Ma - ri* — — — —

a!
a!
a!
a!

dim.

pp

DEDICATION

Widmung

HIGH VOICE

Wolfgang Mueller

Robert Franz
(1815-1892)
ed. KEM

Oh, thank me not for songs I sing thee, Thine are the
O dan - ke nicht für die - se Lie - der, mir ziemt es,

songs, no gift of mine. Thou gav'st them me;⎯ I but re-
dank - bar Dir zu sein; Du gabst sie mir,⎯ ich ge - be

turn thee what now and al - ways will be thine.
wie - der, was jetzt und einst und e - wig Dein.

DEDICATION
Widmung
LOW VOICE

Wolfgang Mueller

Robert Franz
(1815-1892)
ed. KEM

Oh, thank me not for songs I sing thee, Thine are the
O danke nicht für diese Lieder, mir ziemt es,

songs, no gift of mine. Thou gav'st them me; I but re-
dank-bar Dir zu sein; Du gabst sie mir, ich ge-be

turn thee what now and al-ways will be thine.
wie-der, was jetzt und einst und e-wig Dein.

DOWN LOW IN THE VALLEY

Da Unten im Tale

HIGH VOICE

Johannes Brahms
(1833-1897)
ed. KEM

1. Down low in the val - ley the wa - ter is
2. You al - ways speak of love, You al - ways speak of
1. Da un - ten im Ta - le läufts Was - ser so
2. Sprichst all - weil von Lieb. sprichst all - weil von

p dolce

dark, And I can - not say to you how
loy - al - ty, But a lit - tle bit of false - ness, is
trüb und i kann dirs nit sa - gen, i
Treu und a bis - se - le Falsch - heit is

dim.

much I love you.
al - so in you.
hab di so lieb.
au wohl da - bei!

3. And ___ if I _____ tell you how much _____ I
4. I _____ thank you _____ kind - ly for the time that you
3. *Und ___ wenn i dirs zehn - mal sag das i di*
4. *Für die Zeit, wo du g'liebt mi hast, dank i dir*

love you, And you will not be - lieve me, Then
loved me, And I hope that it else - where will
lieb, _____ und du willst nit ver - ste - hen, muss
schön, _____ und i wünsch, dass dirs an - ders - wo

I must move on.
bet - ter be for you.
i halt wei - ter gehn.
bes - ser mag gehn.

DOWN LOW IN THE VALLEY

Da Unten im Tale

LOW VOICE

Johannes Brahms
(1833-1897)
ed. KEM

1. Down low in the val - ley the wa - ter is
2. You al - ways speak of love,——— You al - ways speak of
1. Da —— un - ten im Ta - le läufts Was - ser so
2. Sprichst all - weil von Lieb,——— sprichts all - weil von

dark,——— And I can - not say to you how much I love
loy-al - ty, But a lit - tle bit of false - ness is al - so in
trüb——— und i kann dirs nit sa - gen, i hab di so
Treu——— und a bis - se - le Falsch - heit is au wohl da -

you.
you.
lieb.
bei!

3. And ___ if I ___ tell you how much ___ I
4. I ___ thank you ___ kind - ly for the time that you
3. *Und___ wenn i dirs zehn - mal sag, das i di*
4. *Für die Zeit, wo du g'liebt mi hast, dank i dir*

love you, And you will not be - lieve me, Then I must move
loved me, And I hope that it else - where will bet - ter be for
lieb, ___ und du willst nit ver - ste - hen, muss i halt wei - ter
schön, ___ und i wünsch, dass dirs an - ders - wo bes - ser mag

on.
you.
gehn.
gehn.

FLORIAN'S SONG
Chanson de Florian
HIGH VOICE

J.P. Claris de Florian

Benjamin Godard
(1849-1895)
ed. KEM

1. If there's a shep-herd in your par - ish,
1. *Ah! s'il est dans vo-tre vil - la - ge*

A shep-herd charm - ing, good and kind,
Un ber - ger sen - sible et char - mant,

To whom at
Qu'on ché - risse

once your heart's in - clined, Whom long - er known, still more you cher - ish,
au pre - mier mo - ment, Qu'on aime en - sui - te da - van - ta - ge,

He is my love, Give him to me! I have his heart; __ my
C'est mon a - mi, ren - dez - le moi! J'ai son a - mour, __ il

130

faith has he.
a ma foi.
2. Are echo-ing woods his song re - peat - ing,
2. *Si par sa voix ten-dre et plain-ti - ve,*
Charmed by his voice, that sweet com - plains,
Il char-me l'é-cho de vos bois,
And do his
Si les ac -
pipe's mel - o - dious strains The hearts of maid-ens set a - beat - ing,
cents de son haut - bois Ren-dent la ber-ge-re pen-si - ve,
Then 'tis my love! Give him to me! I have his heart,___ my faith has
C'est en-cor lui, ren-dez-le moi! J'ai son a-mour,___ il a ma

FLORIAN'S SONG
Chanson de Florian
LOW VOICE

J.P. Claris de Florian

Benjamin Godard
(1849-1895)
ed. KEM

1. If there's a shep-herd in your par - ish,
1. *Ah! s'il est dans vo-tre vil-la - ge*

A shep-herd charm-ing, good and kind, To whom at
Un ber - ger sen-sible et char - mant, Qu'on ché-risse

once your heart's in-clined, Whom long-er known, still more you cher - ish,
au pre-mier mo-ment, Qu'on aime en-sui-te da-van-ta - ge,

He is my love, Give him to me! I have his heart; — my
C'est mon a - mi, ren-dez - le moi! J'ai son a-mour, — il

133

faith has he.
a ma foi.

2. Are echo-ing woods his song re - peat -
2. Se par sa voix ten-dre et plain - ti -

ing,
ve,

Charmed by his voice that sweet com-plains,
Il char-me l'é - cho de vos bois,

And do his
Si les ac -

pipe's mel - o-dious strains, The hearts of maid-ens set a beat - ing, Then 'tis my
cents de son haut - bois Ren-dent la ber-ge - re pen - si - ve, C'est en - cor

love! Give him to me! I have his heart,— my faith has he.
lui, ren - dez - le moi! J'ai son a - mour,— il a ma foi.

3. If, when there comes some need-y broth - er, Who begs a
3. *Si pas - sant près de sa chau-miè - re* *Le pauvre, en*

lamb from out the herd, The shep-herd gives with kind-ly word the lit - tle
vo - yant son trou-peau. *O - se de - man - der un a-gneau Et qu'il ob -*

lamb and e'en its moth - er, Oh! then 'tis he!
tienne en - core la mè - re, *Oh! c'est bien lui,*

Give him to me! I have his heart,—— my faith has he.
ren - dez - le moi! *J'ai son a - mour,—— il a ma foi.*

FOLK SONG

Volkslied

HIGH VOICE

Ernst F. von Feuchtersleben

Felix Mendelssohn, Op. 47, No. 4
(1809-1847)
ed. KEM

1. It is or-dain'd by will di-vine, What we love best we
2. If thou dost call one flow'r thine own, One bloom thy yearn-ing
3. And if the Lord hath giv'n a love Thy heart doth prize all

1. *Es ist be-stimmt in Got-tes Rath, dass man vom Lieb-sten,*
2. *So dir ge-schenkt ein Knösp-lein was, so thu' es in ein*
3. *Und hat dir Gott ein Lieb be-scheert, und hälst du sie recht*

must re-sign At part - ing; Al - tho' in all the
heart a-lone Doth cher-ish, When smiles a-rose at
else a-bove, Thy near-est, Too soon shall thou be

was man hat, muss schei-den; wie-wohl doch nichts im
ser-glas, doch wis-se: blüht mor-gen dir ein
in-nig werth, die Dei-ne, es wird nur we-nig

world there's naught So full with pain and sor-row fraught As
morn for thee, As night thou shalt al-read-y see 'Twill
left a-lone Thy loss with mourn-ful tears to moan, Thy

Lauf der Welt dem Her-zen ach! so sau-er fällt, als
Rös-lein auf, es welkt wohl schon die Nacht da-rauf, das
Zeit wohl sein, da lässt sie dich so gar al-lein, dann

136

part - ing: ay, part - ing!
per - ish: ay, per - ish!
dear - est! ay, dear - est!
Schei - den! ja Schei - den!
wis - se! ja wis - se!
wei - ne! ja wei - ne!

4. Yet life and love are not in vain, are not in vain: Tho'
4. *Nun musst du mich auch recht ver-steh'n, ja recht ver-steh'n! Wenn*

part - ing wring the hearts of men, 'Tis then they say: We
Men - schen aus ein - an - der geh'n, So sa - gen sie: auf

meet a - gain! We meet a - gain! We meet a - gain!
Wie - der-seh'n! auf Wie - der-seh'n! auf Wie - der - seh'n!

FOLK SONG

Volkslied

LOW VOICE

Ernst F. von Feuchtersleben

Felix Mendelssohn, Op. 47, No. 4
(1809-1847)
ed. KEM

part - ing: ay,   part -   ing!
per - ish: ay,   per -   ish!
dear - est!   ay,   dear -   est!
Schei - den!   *ja   Schei - den!*
wis - se!   *ja   wis -   se!*
wei - ne!   *ja   wei -   ne!*

4. Yet   life   and   love   are   not   in   vain,   are   not   in   vain: Tho'
4. *Nun   musst   du   mich   auch   recht   ver-steh'n,   ja   recht   ver - steh'n! Wenn*

part - ing   wring   the   hearts   of   men,   'Tis   then   they   say: We
Men - schen   aus   ein - an - der   geh'n,   so   sa - gen   sie: auf

meet   a - gain!   We   meet   a - gain!   We   meet   a - gain!
Wie - der-seh'n!   auf   Wie - der-seh'n!   auf   Wie - der - seh'n!

139

GREENSLEEVES

from the Opera
Sir John in Love

Traditional

Folk tune Arranged by
R. Vaughan Williams

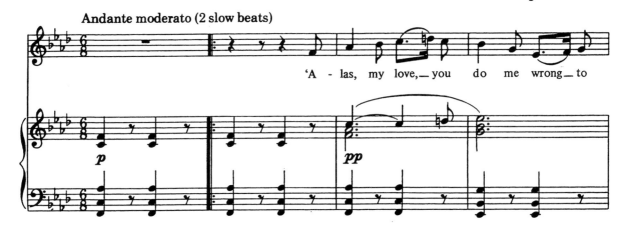

'A - las, my love,— you do me wrong— to

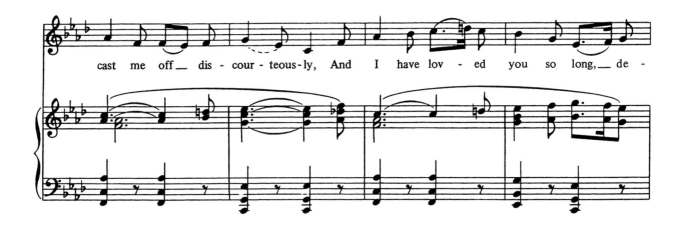

cast me off— dis - cour - teous-ly, And I have lov - ed you so long,— de -

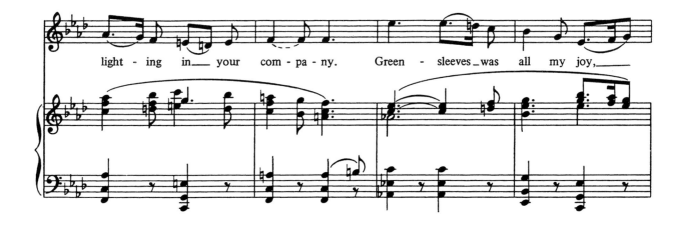

light - ing in— your com - pa - ny. Green - sleeves— was all my joy,—

Green - sleeves was my de-light, Green - sleeves was my heart of gold, and who but my la - dy

Green - sleeves.

2. I have been ready at your hand,
   to grant what ever you would crave;
   I have both waged life and land,
   your love and good will for to have.
   Greensleeves was all my joy, etc.

3. I bought thee kerchers to thy head,
   that were wrought fine and gallantly;
   I kept thee both at board and bed,
   which cost my purse well favouredly.
   Greensleeves was all my joy, etc.

4. I bought thee petticoats of the best,
   the cloth so fine as fine might be;
   I gave thee jewels for thy chest;
   and all this cost I spent on thee.
   Greensleeves was all my joy, etc.

5. Thy girdle of gold so red,
   with pearls bedecked sumptuously;
   The like no other lasses had,
   and yet thou wouldest not love me.
   Greensleeves was all my joy, etc.

6. Thy crimson stockings, all of silk,
   with gold all wrought above the knee;
   Thy pumps, as white as was the milk;
   and yet thou wouldst not love me.
   Greensleeves was all my joy, etc.

7. Thy gown was of the grassy green,
   thy sleeves of satin hanging by,
   Which made thee be our harvest queen;
   and yet thou wouldst not love me.
   Greensleeves was all my joy, etc.

8. Thy garters fringed with the gold,
   and silver aglets hanging by,
   Which made thee blithe for to behold;
   and yet thou wouldst not love me.
   Greensleeves was all my joy, etc.

9. Thou couldst desire no earthly thing,
   but still thou hadst it readily;
   Thy music still to play and sing;
   and yet thou wouldst not love me.
   Greensleeves was all my joy, etc.

10. And who did pay for all this gear,
    that thou didst spend when pleased thee?
    Even I that am rejected here;
    and thou disdainest to love me.
    Greensleeves was all my joy, etc.

11. Well, I will pray to God on high,
    that thou my constancy may'st see;
    For I am still thy lover true;
    come once again, and love me.
    Greensleeves was all my joy, etc.

Version from Clement Robinson's *A Handefull of Pleasant Delites. 1584* (The spelling modernized.)

IF THOU BE NEAR

Bist Du Bei Mir

HIGH VOICE

Johann Sebastian Bach
(1685-1750)
ed. KEM

If thou be near, / Then will I
Bist du bei mir, / *geh' i mit*

fear not to greet my death with grateful heart, to
Freu - den zum Ster - ben und zu mei - ner Ruh', zum

greet my death with grate-ful heart. / If thou be near,
Ster - ben und zu mei-ner Ruh'! / *Bist du bei mir,*

Then will I fear not to greet __ my __ death with grate - ful __
geh' ich mit Freu - den zum Ster - ben __ und zu mei - ner __

heart, to _____ greet my death with grate-ful heart. What sweet con -
Ruh', zum __ Ster - ben und zu mei - ner Ruh' __ Ach, wie ver -

tent to have thee near __ me, with thy __ blest __
gnügt wär' so mein En - de, es drück - ten __

hand up - on __ my __ brow, __ when at __ last my eye - lids close in death.
dei - ne lie - ben __ Hän - de mir __ die ge-treu-en Au - gen zu!

IF THOU BE NEAR

Bist Du Bei Mir

LOW VOICE

Johann Sebastian Bach
(1685-1750)
ed. KEM

If thou be near,
Bist du bei mir,

Then will I fear not to greet__ my__ death with grate - ful__
geh' ich mit Freu - den zum Ster - ben__ und zu mei - ner__

heart, to __ greet my death with grate - ful heart.
Ruh', zum __ Ster - ben und zu mei - ner Ruh'!

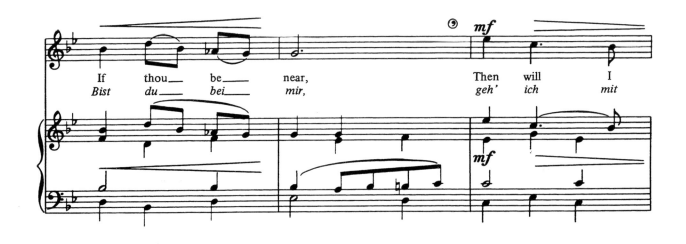

If thou_ be_ near, Then will I
Bist du_ bei_ mir, *geh' ich mit*

fear not to greet_ my_ death with grate - ful_
Freu - den *zum Ster - ben_* *und zu mei - ner_*

heart, to_____ greet my death with grate - ful heart.
Ruh', zum_____ Ster - ben und zu mei - ner Ruh'

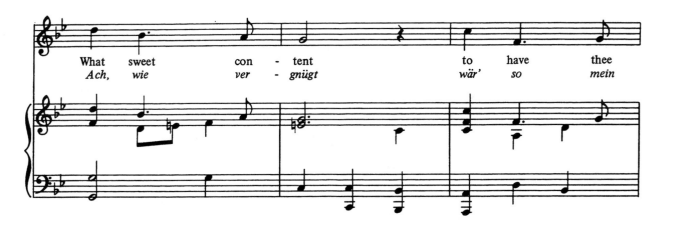

What sweet con - tent to have thee
Ach, wie ver - gnügt wär' so mein

near me, with thy blest hand up - on my
En - de, es drück - ten dei - ne lie - ben

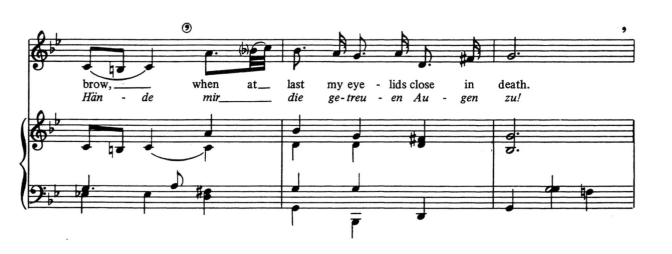

brow, when at last my eye - lids close in death.
Hän - de mir die ge - treu - en Au - gen zu!

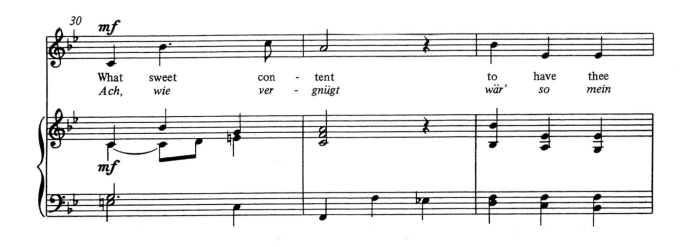

What sweet con - tent to have thee
Ach, wie ver - gnügt wär' so mein

near me, with thy___ blest___ hand up - on___ my___
En - de, es drück - ten___ dei - ne lie - ben___

brow,___ when at___ last my eye - lids close in death.
Hän - de mir_____ die ge-treu - en Au - gen zu!

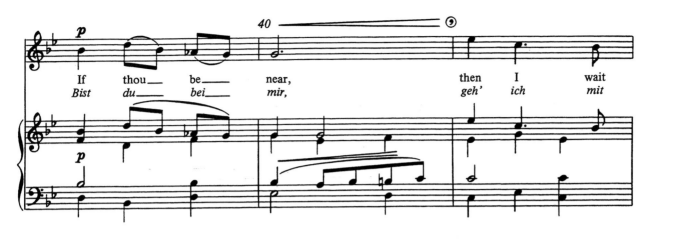

If thou be near, then I wait
Bist du bei mir, geh' ich mit

calm - ly, to greet my death with grate - ful
Freu - den, zum Ster - ben und zu mei - ner

heart, to greet my death with grate - ful heart.
Ruh', zum Ster - ben und zu mei - ner Ruh'!

IT WAS A LOVER AND HIS LASS

HIGH VOICE

William Shakespeare

Thomas Morley
(1557-1603)
ed. KEM

1. It was a lov - er and his lass,
2. Be - tween the a - cres of the rye,
3. This car - ol they be - gan that hour,
4. Then, pret - ty lov - ers, take the time,

With a

hey, with a ho, with a hey, non - ne - no, And a hey, _____

_____ non - ne - no, ne - no!

That o'er the green corn - field did pass,
These pret - ty coun - try fools did lie
Of how that life was but a flow'r
For love is crown - ed with the prime,

In

IT WAS A LOVER AND HIS LASS

LOW VOICE

William Shakespeare

Thomas Morley
(c. 1557-1603)
ed. KEM

1. It was a lov - er and his lass,
2. Be - tween the a - cres of the rye,
3. This car - ol they be - gan that hour,
4. Then, pret - ty lov - ers, take the time,

With a hey, with a ho, with a hey, non - ne - no, And a hey, _____ non - ne - no, ne - no!

That o'er the green corn - field did pass,
These pret - ty coun - try fools did lie
Of how that life was but a flow'r
For love is crown - ed with the prime,

With a

In

152

spring - time, in spring - time, in spring - time, The on - ly pret - ty

ring - time, When birds do sing, Hey ding a ding a ding, Hey

ding a ding a ding, Hey ding a ding a ding, Sweet lov - ers love the spring.

THE LASS WITH THE DELICATE AIR

Michael Arne
ed. KEM

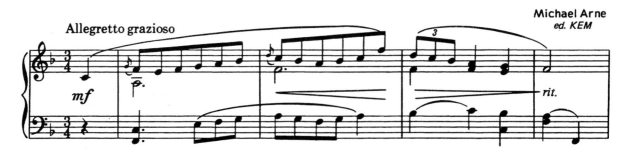

1. Young Mol - ly who__ lived at the foot__ of __ the__ hill, Whose
2. One eve - ning last___ May, as I trav - ersed_ the__ grove, In

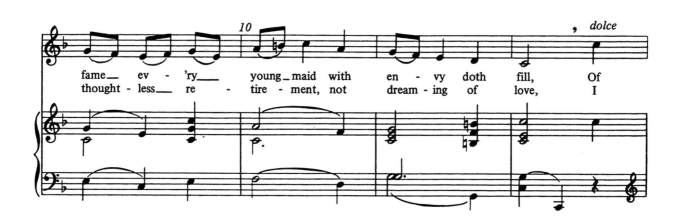

fame_ ev - 'ry__ young_ maid with en - vy doth fill, Of
thought - less__ re - tire - ment, not dream - ing of love, I

beau - ty___ is___ bless'd with__ so___ am - ple__ a___ share,___ Men
chanced to__ es - py the___ gay nymph, I__ de - clare,___ And

call her__ the___ lass with the del - i - cate air, with the
real - ly___ she__ had a most del - i - cate air, a most

del - - - - - i - cate air,___ Men
del - - - - - i - cate air,___ And

call__ her__ the___ lass__ with__ the___ del - i - cate air.
real - ly___ she__ had a___ most del - i - cate air.

mp 3. By a   mur - mur - ing___ brook, on   a   green__ moss - y___
mf 4. A___   thou - sand times___ o'er I've   re - peat - ed___ my

knoll,   A   chap - let__ com - pos - ing, the   fair__ maid   lay   still;   Sur -
suit,   But   still__ the__ tor - men - tor af - fects__ to   be   mute!   Then

prised and__ trans - port - ed__ I___ could   not__ for - bear___ With__
tell   me   ye___ swains who   have__ con - quered__ the__ fair,___ How   to

rap - ture__ to___ gaze   on   her   del - i - cate   air,   on   her
win   the__ dear__ lass   with   the   del - i - cate   air,   with   the

mf

156

del - - - - i-cate air,___ With ___
del - - - - i-cate air,___ How to

rap-ture to___ gaze___ on___ her del-i-cate___ air.

win ___ the dear ___ lass ___ with ___ the ___ del-i-cate ___ air.

LOVE HAS EYES

HIGH VOICE

Charles Dibdin

Sir Henry Rowley Bishop
(1786-1855)
ed. KEM

* This note is to be played the second time only.

LOVE HAS EYES
LOW VOICE

Charles Dibdin

Sir Henry Rowley Bishop
(1786-1855)
ed. KEM

1. Love's blind they say, ___ O nev - er nay, ___ Can words ___ love's ___ grace ___ im - part, ___ The fan - cy weak, ___ The tongue may speak, ___

2. Love's wing'd they cry, ___ O nev - er I ___ No pin - ions ___ have ___ to ___ soar, ___ De - ceiv - ers rove, ___ But nev - er love, ___

But eyes____ a - lone the heart,
At - tach'd,__ he __ roves no more!

In one soft look what lan - guage
Can he have wings who nev - er

lies, O yes, be - lieve me, Love has
flies? And yes, be - lieve me, Love has

eyes, O __ love has __ eyes, __ Love has eyes,__ O __
eyes, O __ love has __ eyes, __

*This note is to be played the second time only.

MAY-DAY CAROL

English Folk song (Essex)
Transcribed and Harmonized by
DEEMS TAYLOR
Op. 15, No. 9

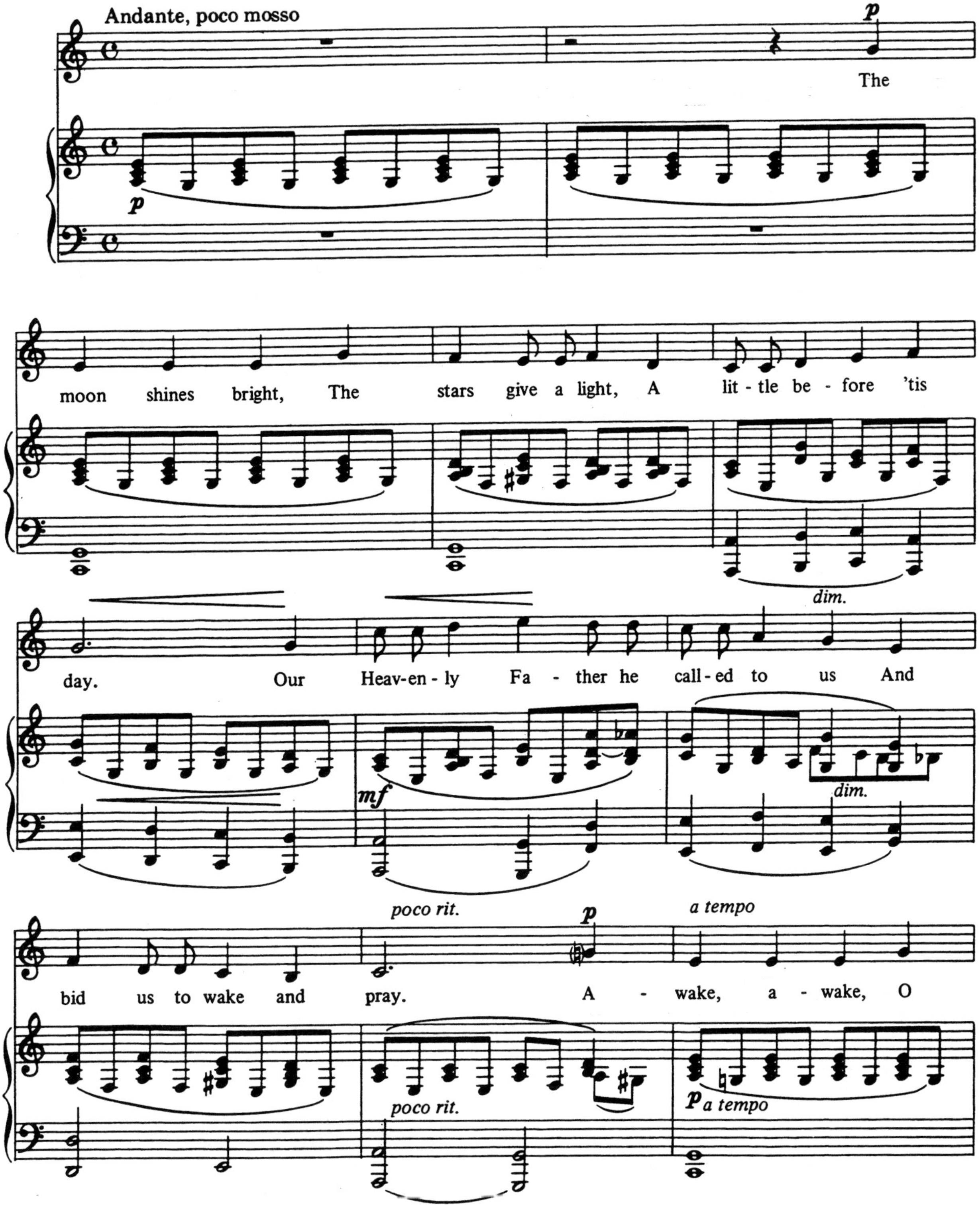
Andante, poco mosso
p
The
p
moon shines bright, The stars give a light, A lit - tle be - fore 'tis
dim.
day. Our Heav-en - ly Fa - ther he call - ed to us And
mf
dim.
poco rit.
p
a tempo
bid us to wake and pray. A - wake, a - wake, O
poco rit.
p a tempo

pret - ty, pret - ty maid, Out of your drows - y dream, And step in - to your dair - y be - low, And fetch me a bowl of cream. not a bowl of your sweet cream, *Or:* (A mug of your brown

If

A mug cup of to your bring brown me

rit. *p* *rit.* *a tempo* *a tempo*

For the Lord knows where we shall meet a-gain To be

(beer; cheer;)

may-ing an-oth-er year. I been a-ram-bling

all this night, And some time of this day, And

now, re-turn-ing back a-gain, I brought you a branch of May.

appassionato

cresc.

_f_ molto dim.

pp _a tempo_

A branch of May I brought you here, And

p rit. **pp** _a tempo_

_mf_

at your door I stand. 'Tis noth-ing but a sprout, but

cresc. _mf_

dim. rall. **p**

well bud-ded out By the work of Our Lord's hand. My

dim. rall.

MY HEART NE'ER LEAPS WITH GLADNESS

Nel cor più non mi sento

Translation by*
James P. Dunn

Giovanni Paisiello
(1741-1816)
ed. KEM

My heart ne'er leaps with glad - ness, Youth's glow it ___ feels_ no
Nel cor più non mi sen - to bril - lar la ___ gio - ven -

more, All full of woe ___ and sad - ness, 'Tis
tù; ca - gion del mio ___ tor - men - to, a -

*"English Singing Translations of Foreign Language Art Songs," *National Association of Teachers of Singing,* 1976. Used by permission.

Love the fault_ must bear. He nips at me, he nudg-es me. He
mor, sei col - pa tu. Mi piz - zi - chi, mi stuz-zi-chi, mi

nee - dles me, he pinch-es me, Ah, me, what can _ I do? _ Ah
pun - gi - chi, mi mas - ti - chi; che co - sa è que - sto ahi - mè? _ pie -

love,_ have care,_ have care!_ 'Tis you, in - deed,_ I know, _____ That_
tà, _ pie - tà, _ pie - tà! _ a - mo re è un cer - to che, _____ che _

caus - es my__ de - spair.
di - spe - rar_ mi fa.

MY LOVELY CELIA

HIGH VOICE

George Monro
ed. KEM

My love - ly Ce - lia, heav'n - ly fair, As li - lies sweet, as soft as

air, No more,— then, tor - ment — me,

but _____ be ____ kind, And with _____ your ____

love __ ease my trou - bled mind.

O, let _____ me ____

171

gaze _____ on your _____ bright _____ eyes, Where melt - ing _____

beams so oft _____ a - rise, My heart's _____ en -

chant - ed with _____ thy _____ charms, Oh, take _____ me, _____

dy - ing, to _____ your arms. _____

MY LOVELY CELIA

LOW VOICE

George Monro
ed. KEM

lovely Celia, heav'nly fair, As lil-lies sweet, as soft as

gaze ___ on your ___ bright ___ eyes, Where melt - ing ___

beams so oft ___ a - rise, My heart's ___ en -

chant - ed with ___ thy ___ charms, Oh, take ___ me, ___

dy - ing, to ___ your arms. ___

NINA
HIGH VOICE

Giovanni B. Pergolesi
(1710-1736)
ed. KEM

Andante

'Tis_ three long days that Ni - na, my Ni - na, my Ni - na, In
Tre — gior - ni son che Ni - na, che Ni - na, che Ni - na, in

slum - ber soft and deep, _____ in _ slum - ber _ soft and deep.
let - to se ne sta, _____ in _ let - to _ se ne sta.

Cym-bals and flutes_ and trum-pets sound! A - wak - en Ni-net - ta, a-
Pif - fa - ri, tim - pa-ni, cem - ba - li, sve - glia - te mia Ni-net - ta, sve-

NINA

LOW VOICE

Giovanni B. Pergolesi
(1710-1736)
ed. KEM

wak - en Ni - net - ta, I pray you no more sleep, _____ I _____
glia - te mia Ni - net - ta, ac - ciò non dor - ma più, _____ ac -

pray_ you_ no more sleep. A - wak - en_ my_ Ni - net - ta, a -
ciò_ non dor - ma più; sve - glia - te_ mia_ Ni - net - ta, sve -

wak - en_ my_ Ni - net - ta, I pray_ you_ no_ more_ sleep.
glia - te mia_ Ni - net - ta, ac - ciò_ non dor - ma_ più.

sleep, I pray you no _____ more sleep.
più, ac - ciò non dor - ma piu.

O RELENT, NO MORE TORMENT ME
O cessate di piagarmi
HIGH VOICE

Translated by*
James P. Dunn

Alessandro Scarlatti
(1659-1725)
ed. KEM

*"English Singing Translations of Foreign Language Art Songs," National Association of Teachers of Singing, 1976. Used by permission.

spite - ful, hate - ful, Cold as ice and cold as mar - ble.
and dis - dain - ful, You can ease me, heal and cleanse me,
di - spie - ta - te, più del ge - lo e più di mar - mi
or - go - glio - si, voi po - te - te ri - sa - nar - mi

Cold and deaf to my tor - tured cry! Cold and deaf to my
Yet you joy in my tor - tured cry! Yet you joy in my
fred - dee sor - dea' miei mar - tir, fred - dee sor - dea'
e go - de - te al mio lan - guir, e go - de - te al

tor - tured cry! O re - lent, no more tor - ment me,
tor - tured cry! Worse than an - y asp or vi - per,
miei — mar - tir. O ces - sa - te di pia - gar - mi,
mio — lan - guir.

O, I pray you, let me die, O, I pray you, let me die.
Harsh and heed - less to my sighs, Harsh and heed - less to my sighs!
O la - scia - te - mi mo - rir, O la - scia - te - mi mo - rir.

O RELENT, NO MORE TORMENT ME

O cessate di piagarmi

LOW VOICE

Translated by*
James P. Dunn

Alessandro Scarlatti
(1660-1725)
ed. KEM

⑨

Andantino — mf

1. O re - lent, no more tor - ment me,
2. Worse than an - y asp or vi - per,
1. O ces - sa - te di pia - gar - mi,
2. Piu d'un an - gue, piu d'un a - spe

O, I pray you, let me die! O, I pray you, let me die!
Harsh and heed - less to my sighs! Harsh and heed - less to my sighs!
O la - scia - te - mi mo - rir, O la - scia - te - mi mo - rir.
cru - die sor - dia miei so spir, cru - die sor - dia miei so spir,

Eyes un - grate - ful, spite - ful, hate - ful, Eyes un - grate - ful,
Eyes so bane - ful and dis - dain - ful, Eyes so bane - ful
Lu - c'in - gra - te, di - spie - ta - te, lu - c'in - gra - te,
Oc - chia - tro - ci, or - go - glio - si, oc - chia - tro - ci

*"English Singing Translations of Foreign Language Art Songs," *National Association of Teachers of Singing,* 1976. Used by permission.

O'ER THE GANGES NOW RISES

Già il sole dal Gange

HIGH VOICE

Alessandro Scarlatti
(1660-1725)
ed. KEM

Allegro giusto (♩ = 126)

mf *brillante*

1. O'er the Gan - ges____ now____ ris - es, o'er the Gan - ges now
rays____ gold - en____ beam - ing, his rays gold - en
1. *Già il so - le____ dal____ Gan - ge, Già il so - le dal*
rag - gio____ do - ra - to, col rag - gio do -

ris - es, now ris - es, now ris - es in splen - dor, now ris - es in
beam - ing de - pose,____ de - pose night - ly shad - ows, de - pose night - ly
Gan - ge più chia - ro, più chia - ro sfa - vil - la più chia - ro sfa -
ra - to, col rag - gio do - ra - to in gem - ma, in gem - ma o - gni

leggero

tr

184

splen - dor, the sun - god, the sun - god in splen - dor,
shad - ows, de - pose, ___ de - pose night - ly shad - ows,
vil - la, più chia - ro, più chia - ro sfa - vil - la,
ste - lo, in gem - ma, in gem - ma o - gni ste - la,

poco rit.

20 a tempo

With dew - drops all gleam - ing the morn he ___ a -
While all through the mead - ows with stars bright - ly ___
e ter - ge o - gni stil - la del l'al - ba ___ che ___
e gli as - tri del cie - lo di - pin - ge ___ nel ___

25

pp   cresc. poco a poco e legatiss.

wak - ens,   With dew - drops all gleam - ing the morn he a -
beam - ing,   While all through the mead - ows with stars bright - ly
pian - ge,   del l'al - be che pian - ge, del l'al - ba che
pra - to,   di - pin - ge nel pra - to, di - pin - ge nel

p

cresc. poco a poco e legatiss.

185

wak - ens, with dew-drops all gleam - ing. ____
beam - ing, the dew-drops are gleam - ing bright. ____
pian - ge, del l'al - ba che pian - ge. ____
pra - to, di - pin - ge nel pra - to. ____

O'er the Gan - ges ____ now ____ ris - es, o'er the Gan - ges now
His rays ____ gold - en beam - ing, his rays gold - en
Già il so - le dal ____ Gan - ge, già il so - le dal
Col rag - gio ____ do - ra - to, col rag - gio do -

ris - es, now ris - es, now ris - es in splen - dor, now
beam - ing de - pose, ____ de - pose night - ly shad - ows, de -
Gan - ge più chia - ro, più chia - ro sfa - vil - la, più
ra - to, in gem - ma, in gem - ma o - gni ste - lo, in

ris - es   in   splen - dor, the   sun - god,   the   sun - god in
pose night - ly shad - ows, de - pose,___ de - pose night - ly
chia - ro   sfa - vil - la,   più   chia - ro,   più   chia - ro sfa -
gem - ma o - gni   ste - lo,   in   gem - ma o - gni ste - lo,   in

splen - dor.
shad - ows.
vil - la.
ste - lo.

2. His
2. Col

O'ER THE GANGES NOW RISES

Già il sole dal Gange
LOW VOICE

Alessandro Scarlatti
(1660-1725)
ed. KEM

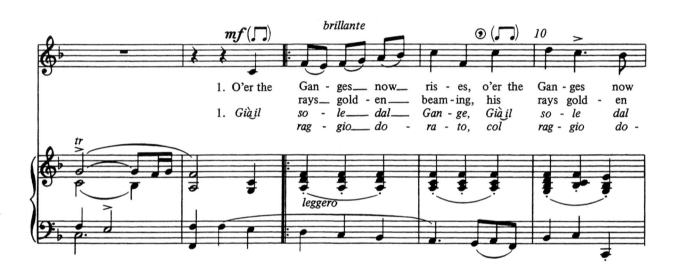

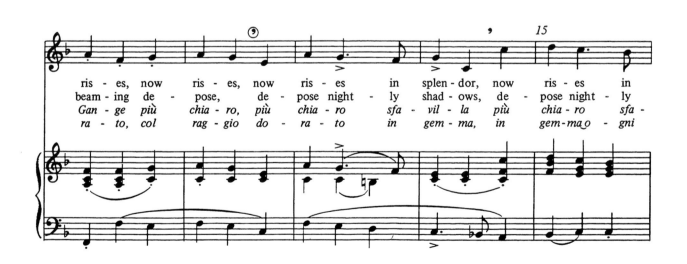

ris - es   in   splen - dor,   the   sun - god,   the   sun - god   in
pose night - ly   shad - ows, de - pose,   de - pose   night - ly
chia - ro   sfa - vil - la, più chia - ro,   più   chia - ro   sfa
gem - ma o - gni   ste - lo, in - gem - ma o - gni   ste - lo,   in -

splen - dor.
shad - ows.
vil - la.
ste - lo.

1.   2.   2. His
            2. Col

ON A CLEAR DAY
(You Can See Forever)

Words by
Alan Jay Lerner

Music by
Burton Lane

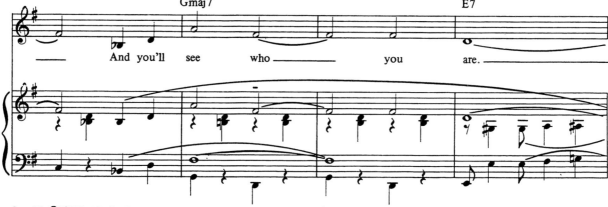

PASSING BY

HIGH VOICE

Words from Thomas Ford's
Musicke of Sundrie Kinds (1607)

Edward Purcell
(1689-1740)
ed. KEM

till I die.

3. Cu - pid is wing - ed and doth range her coun - try,

so my love ─── doth change, But change ─── the earth, or

change the sky, Yet will I love her till I die.

PASSING BY
LOW VOICE

Words from Thomas Ford's
Musicke of Sundrie Kinds (1607)

Edward Purcell
(1689-1740)
ed. KEM

198

till I die.

3. Cu - pid is wing - ed and doth range her coun - try,

so my love____ doth change, But change____ the earth, or

change the sky, Yet will I love her till I die.

DOWN BY THE SALLY GARDENS

Old Irish Song, new words by W.B. Yeats
This arrangement by T.C. Kelly

lit - tle — snow white feet. She bid me — take love eas - - y, As the leaves grow — on — the — tree, But — I be - ing young and — fool - ish with — her did — not a - gree.

In a field down by the river my love and I did stand,
And on my leaning shoulder, she laid her snow-white hand.
She bid me take life easy, as the grass grows on the weirs;
But I was young and foolish, and now am full of tears.

SEE THE SUN'S CLEAR RAYS

Come raggio di sol
HIGH VOICE

Translation by
James P. Dunn*

Antonio Caldara
(1670-1763)
ed. KEM

See _____ the sun's clear rays. Radiant and lus - trous.
Co - me rag - gio di sol mi - te e se - re - no,

See _____ the sun's clear rays. Radiant and lus - trous
co - me rag - gio di sol mi - te e se - re - no

Dance and play on the bil - lows gent-ly surg - ing,
so - vra pla - ci - di flut - ti si ri - po - sa,

*"English Singing Translations of Foreign Language Art Songs," *National Association of Teachers of Singing*, 1976. Used by permission.

While far be-low them, far,＿ far be-low them, Bur-ied
men - tre del ma - re, men - tre del ma - re nel pro-

deep and sun - less, A hid-den tem - -
fon - do se - no sta la tem - pe - -

- - pest is rag - - ing;
- - sta a sco - - sa:

E - ven so, tho' on my face a smile be creep - ing, Sweet con-
co - si ri - só ta - lor ga-io e pa - ca - to di con-

tent - ment, a mask of pure en - joy - ment,
ten - to, *di gio - ia un lab - bro in - fio - ra,*

While in its se - cret cham - bers, the weep - ing heart
men - tre nel suo se - gre - to il cor pia - ga -

stent.

lies in grief and woe and tor - - -
to s'an - go - scia e si mar - to - - -

ment.
ra.

SEE THE SUN'S CLEAR RAYS

Come raggio di sol
LOW VOICE

Translation by*
James P. Dunn

Antonio Caldara
(1670-1763)
-ed. KEM

See ___ the sun's clear rays. Radiant and lus - trous.
Co - me rag - gio di sol mi - te e se - re - no,

See ___ the sun's clear rays. Radiant and lus - trous.
co - me rag - gio di sol mi - te e se - re - no

Dance and play on the bil - lows gen - tly surg - ing,
so - vra pla - ci - di flut - ti si ri - po - sa,

*"English Singing Translations of Foreign Language Art Songs," *National Association of Teachers of Singing,* 1976. Used by permission.

SERENADE
Ständchen

Franz Schubert
(1797-1828)
ed. KEM

208

Hear_the night - in - gales' sweet mu - sic, Ah, they plead_for me.
Hörst_die Nach - ti - gal - len schla - gen? ach! sie fle - hen dich.

With_their tones so clear,_so mourn - ful,
mit_der Tö - ne sü - ssen Kla - gen

They im - plore __ thee.
fle - hen sie für mich.

They know well a heart's true long - ing, Know 'tis pain to part.
Sie ver-steh'n des Bu - sens Seh - nen, ken -nen Lie - bes - schmerz,

Know 'tis pain to part, Touch with sil - ver-throat - ed voi - ces:
ken - nen Lie - bes - schmerz, rüh - ren mit den Sil - ber-tö - nen

Calm each ach - ing heart, Calm each ach - ing heart.
je - des wei - che Herz, je - des wei - che Herz.

Let thy heart, my dear, grow ten - der. Lis - ten now to me.
Lass auch dir die Brust be - we - gen. Lieb - chen, hö - re mich.

SOMETIMES I FEEL LIKE A MOTHERLESS CHILD

Negro Spiritual

Arranged by
H. T. Burleigh

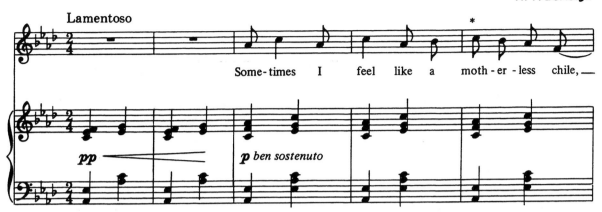

Lamentoso

Some-times I feel like a moth-er-less chile, ___

Some-times I feel like a moth-er-less chile, ___

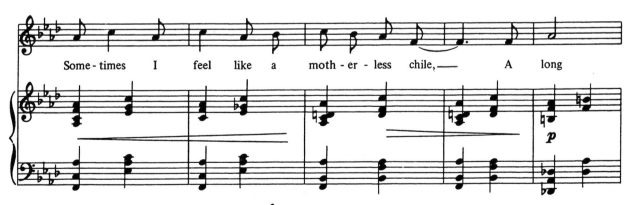

Some-times I feel like a moth-er-less chile, ___ A long

* The original form of this measure was written [music notation] . In order to facilitate vocalization I have taken the liberty of altering it

as above. *H. T. B.*

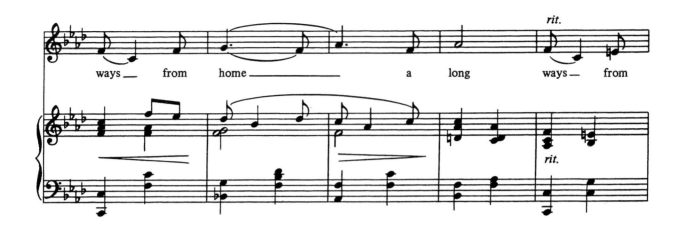

ways ___ from home _____ a long ways ___ from

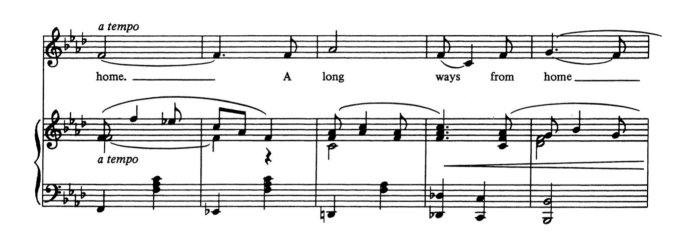

home. _____ A long ways from home _____

___ a long ways ___ from home. _____

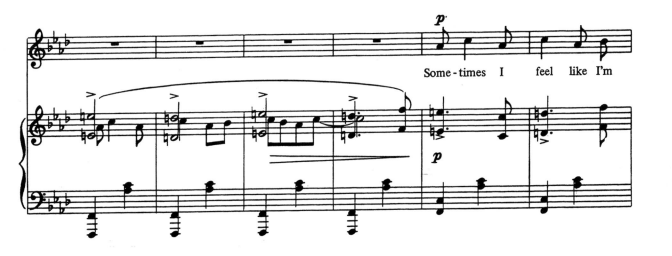

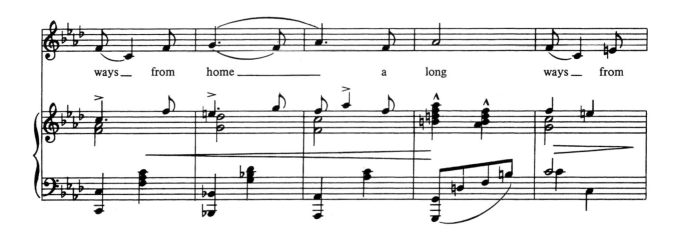

ways__ from home _____ a long ways__ from

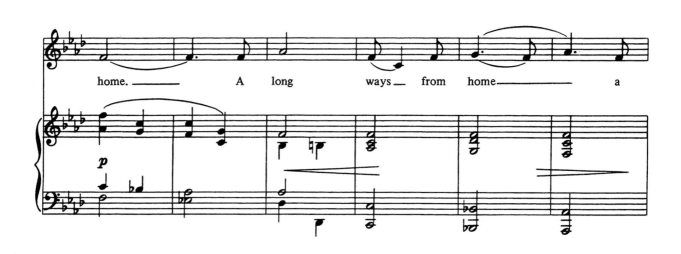

home. _____ A long ways__ from home_____ a

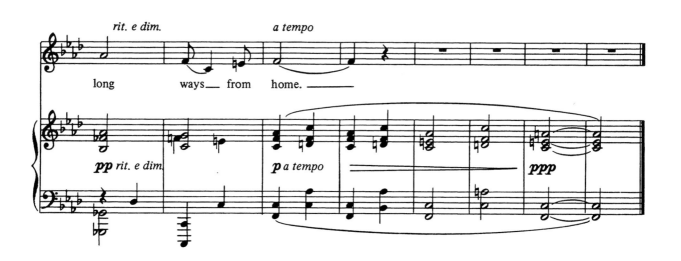

long ways__ from home. _____

THOU ART REPOSE
Du bist die Ruh'

Translation by
Frederic Kirchberger*

Franz Schubert
(1797-1828)
ed. KEM

Thou art re-pose, In-car-nate
Du bist die Ruh', des Frie - de

peace, In these my woes And yearn - ing cease;
mild, die Sehn - sucht du, und was sie stillt;

Dwell thou in me, My in-most part; I of - fer
Ich wei - he dir voll Lust und Schmerz, zur Weh - nung

*"English Singing Translations of Foreign Language Art Songs," *National Association of Teachers of Singing*, 1976. Used by permission.

thee _____ My__ eye__ and __ heart. _____ My__ eye__ and ___ heart. _____
hier _____ *mein_Aug'_ und* ____ *Herz,* _____ *mein_Aug'_ und* ___ *Herz.* _____

This, home is thine For ev - er - more; En - ter the
Kehr' ein bei mir, und schlie - sse du still hin - ter

shrine And close the door. Let pain de - part _____
dir Die Pfor - ten zu. Treib' an - dern Schmerz _____

Far from my sight, Glad be this heart With thy de-
aus die - ser Brust, voll sei dies Herz, von dei - ner

light. With thy de - light.
Lust, von dei - ner Lust.

This ho - ly shrine, By
Dies Au - gen - zelt, von

thy pure flame A - glow with light.
dei - nem Glanz al - lein er - hellt,

TO BE NEAR THEE

Star vicino

HIGH VOICE

Salvator Rosa
(1615-1673)
ed. KEM

near thee, my own true be - lov - ed
ci - no al bel - l'i - dol, che s'a - ma.

Is the joy and de -
E il più va - go di -

joy and de- light __ of my heart. __
va- go di- let- to d'a- mor! __

Tempo primo

To be
Star lon-

far from your own fair be- lov- ed Is the
ta- no dal ben che si bra- ma È d'a-

deep- est grief love doth __ im- part, Is the
mo- re il più vi- vo __ do- lor, È d'a-

TO BE NEAR THEE

Star vicino

LOW VOICE

Salvator Rosa
(1615-1673)
ed. KEM

Andante con moto

To be
Star vi

near thee, my own true be - lov - ed   Is the joy and de -
ci - no al bel - l'i - dol, che s'a - ma,   E il più va - go di -

225

joy and de - light_ of my heart. _____
va - go di - let - to d'a - mor! _____

To be
Star lon -

far from your own fair be - lov - ed Is the
ta - no dal ben che si bra - ma, È d'a -

deep - est grief love doth_ im - part, Is the
mo - re il più vi - vo_ do - lor, È d'a -

TO MUSIC
An die Musik
HIGH VOICE

Franz Schubert, Op. 88, No. 4
(1797-1828)
ed. KEM

heart,___ en - flamed with warm-er___ glad - ness, hast raised my soul to a
Herz ___ zu war - mer Lieb ent - zun - den, hast mich in ei - ne

bet - ter, bet - ter world, hast raised my soul to a bet - ter world!
bess - re Welt ent - rückt, in ei - ne bess - re Welt___ ent - rückt!

Oft now a
Oft hat ein

sigh from out thy harp___been___ flow - ing, a sweet - er
Seuf - zer, dei - ner Harf___ent - flos - sen, ein sü - sser,

chord, a ho - lier word— from— thee.
hei - li-ger Ak - kord— von— dir

A bright - er
den Him - mel

day,___ heav'n's gates to me — are o - pen, Oh love - ly muse, my—
bess - rer— Zei - ten mir er - schloss - en, du hol - de Kunst, ich—

cresc.

(♩ ♩)

thanks I give to thee, I give my thanks— my thanks— to thee!
dan - ke dir da - für, de hol-de Kunst,— ich dan - ke dir!

p

fp   fp

TO MUSIC

An die Musik

LOW VOICE

Franz Schubert, Op. 88, No. 4
(1797-1828)
ed. KEM

THE TURTLE DOVE

HIGH VOICE

English Folk Song
ed. KEM

done. 4. O yon-der doth sit that lit-tle tur-tle dove, He doth sit on yon-der high tree, A mak-ing a moan for the loss of his love, As I will do for thee, my dear, As I will do for thee.

THE TURTLE DOVE

LOW VOICE

English Folk Song
ed. KEM

Andante sostenuto

p

p 1. Fare thee well, my dear, I must be__ gone, And__ leave you__ for a__
mp 2. So__ fair thou art my bon - ny lass, So__ deep in__ love am__
mp 3. The__ sea will nev-er run dry my__ dear, Nor the rocks nev - er melt with the

p

while; For__ though I__ go I'll__ come_ back a - gain, Though I
I; But I nev - er will prove false to the bon-ny lass I love, Till the
sun, But I nev - er will prove false to the bon-ny lass I love, Till__

1.-2.

roam ten thou - sand miles, my dear, Though I roam ten thou - sand miles.
stars fall from the sky, my dear, Till the stars fall from the sky.
all these things be done, my dear, Till__ all these things be

done. 4. O___ yon - der doth sit that lit - tle tur - tle dove, He doth

sit on___ yon - der high tree, A - mak - ing a moan for the

loss of his love, As___ I will do for thee, my dear, As___

I will do for thee.___

238

WHAT IF A DAY

Popular Seventeenth-Century Song

HIGH VOICE

Attributed to
Thomas Campion
(1567 -1620)
ed. KEM

May not the change of a night or an hour / Cross thy de-lights with as many sad tor-ment-ings, as man-y sad tor-ment-ings?

Shall then the point of a point be so vain, / As to tri-umph in a sil-ly point's ad-ven-ture, a sil-ly point's ad-ven-ture?

May not the world by a check of that wealth, / Bring thee a-gain to as low de-spis-ed chang-ing, as low de-spis-ed chang-ing?

For-tune, hon-our, beau-ty,— youth, / Are but blos-soms dy-ing;

All is haz-ard that we— have, / Here is noth-ing bid-ing;

While the sun of wealth doth— shine, / Thou shalt have friends plen-ty;

Wan-ton plea-sures dot-ing— love,

Days of plea-sure are as— streams

But come want, they re-pine,

Are   but shad - ows   fly -   ing.   All   our joys
Thro'   fair mead - ows   glid -   ing.   Weal   or woe,
Not   one a - bides of   twen -   ty!   Wealth   and friends,

are   but toys,   I -   dle thoughts de - ceiv -   ing,
time   doth go,   Time   hath no   re - turn -   ing;
holds   and ends   As   thy for - tunes — rise and   fall;

None   hath pow'r   of   an hour   Of   his life's be - reav -   ing.
Se - cret fates   guide   our states Both   in mirth and — mourn -   ing.
Up   and down,   smile   and frown, Cer -   tain is   no — state at all.

WHAT IF A DAY

Popular Seventeenth-Century Song

LOW VOICE

Attributed to
Thomas Campion
(1567-1620)
ed. KEM

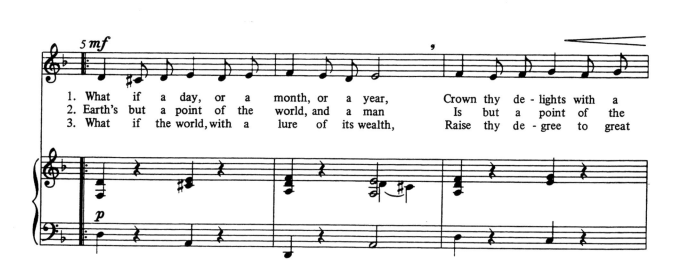

1. What if a day, or a month, or a year, Crown thy de-lights with a
2. Earth's but a point of the world, and a man Is but a point of the
3. What if the world, with a lure of its wealth, Raise thy de-gree to great

thou-sand sweet con - tent - ings, a thou - sand sweet con - tent - ings?
Earth's com-par - ed cen - tre, the Earth's com - par - ed cen - tre:
place of high ad - vanc - ing? great place of high ad - vanc - ing?

242

May not the change of a night or an hour   Cross thy de-lights with as
Shall then the point of a point be so vain,   As to tri-umph in a
May not the world by a check of that wealth,   Bring thee a-gain to as

man-y sad tor-ment-ings, as man-y sad tor-ment-ings?
sil-ly point's ad-ven-ture, a sil-ly point's ad-ven-ture?
low de-spis-ed chang-ing? as low de-spis-ed chang-ing?

For-tune, hon-our, beau-ty, youth,   Are but blos-soms
All is haz-ard that we have,   Here is noth-ing
While the sun of wealth doth shine,   Thou shalt have friends

dy-ing;   Wan-ton pleas-ures dot-ing love,
bid-ing;   Days of pleas-ure are as streams
plen-ty;   But come want, they re-pine,

WHERE'ER YOU WALK

(Aria from Semele)

HIGH VOICE

George Frideric Handel
(1685-1759)
ed. KEM

to _____ a shade.

Wher - e'er you walk, cool gales shall fan the _ glade;

Trees where you sit, shall crown in - to a _ shade. _____

Trees, where you _ sit, shall crowd _____ in -

WHERE'ER YOU WALK
(Aria from Semele)
LOW VOICE

George Frideric Handel
(1685-1759)
ed. KEM

WHO IS SYLVIA

An Sylvia

HIGH VOICE

Franz Schubert
(1797-1828)
ed. KEM

Ho - ly, fair and wise is she;
Love doth to her eyes re - pair,
She ex - cels each mor - tal thing
Schön und zart Seh' ich sie nahn
ih rem Aug' eilt A - mor zu,
Je - den Reiz be - siegt sie lang,

The heav'ns such grace did lend her,
To help him of his blind - ness;
Up - on the dull earth dwell - ing;
auf Him - mels Gunst und Spur weist.
dort heilt er sei - ne Blind - heit.
den Er - de kann - ge - wäh - ren;

That she might ad - in-
And be - ing help'd
To her let us
dass ihr Al - les in
und ver - weilt
Krän - ze ihr und

pp

WHO IS SYLVIA
An Sylvia
LOW VOICE

Franz Schubert
(1797-1828)
ed. KEM

1. Who is Syl - via, What is
2. Is she kind, as she is
3. Then to Syl - via, let us
1. *Was ist Syl - via, sa - get*
2. *Ist sie schön und gut da -*
3. *Da - rum Syl - via, tön, o*

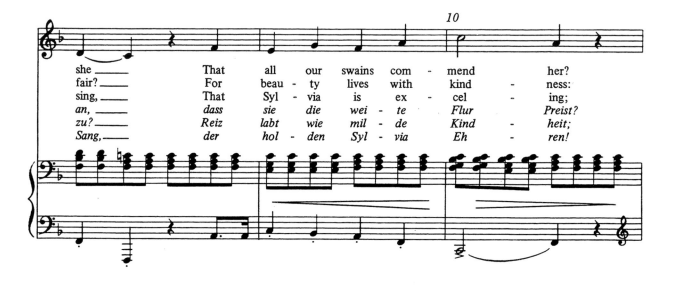

she That all our swains com - mend her?
fair? For beau - ty lives with kind - ness:
sing, That Syl - via is ex - cel - ing;
an, dass sie die wei - te Flur Preist?
zu? Reiz labt wie mil - de Kind - heit;
Sang, der hol - den Syl - via Eh - ren!

mir - ed be, ____ That she
hab - its there, ____ And be - ing
gar - lands bring, ____ To her
un - ter - than, ____ dass ihr
sü - sser Ruh', ____ und ver -
Sai - ten - klang, ____ Krän - ze

25

might ad - mir - ed be.
help'd in hab - its there.
let us gar - lands bring.
Al - les un - ter - than.
weilt in sü - sser Ruh'.
ihr und Sai - ten - klang!

30

Index

* Prevention of vocal disorders

mucous covers internal structures of body

larynx = voice box - sound source

pharynx = nasal cavaties

Nodules - bumps on throat - worst case

Be Aware! Vocal Hygiene.
- if you have an infection - antibiotics
- allergies
- acid reflux - avoid acidic foods
                  papaya enzyme

+ when vomitting don't drink milk afterwards.
        lactaid

How to avoid problems w/ your voice
- keep risky voice to a minimum
- don't over sing - don't give more than you can give
- avoid consuming foods that irritate your voice
        caffeine
        ~~Chocolate~~ Chocolate
        Dairy

- drink juice & water
- use good voice production

know your voice:
pay attention
your speaking
voice as well.

You need to know the symptoms:
        - increased effort required for singing
        - deterioration of nice soft high notes
        - loss of endurance
        - breathiness or increased tendency to run out of air
        - day to day variability